# COMPREHENSION STRATEGIES
## *for Your K–6*
## *Literacy Classroom*

# COMPREHENSION STRATEGIES
## *for Your K-6 Literacy Classroom*

### Thinking Before, During, and After Reading

DIVONNA M. STEBICK          JOY M. DAIN

**CORWIN PRESS**
A SAGE Publications Company
Thousand Oaks, CA 91320

*For information:*

Corwin Press
A Sage Publications Company
2455 Teller Road
Thousand Oaks, California 91320
www.corwinpress.com

Sage Publications Ltd.
1 Oliver's Yard
55 City Road
London EC1Y 1SP
United Kingdom

Sage Publications India Pvt. Ltd.
B-42, Panchsheel Enclave
Post Box 4109
New Delhi 110 017  India

Sage Publications Asia-Pacific Pte Ltd
33 Pekin Street #02-01
Far East Square
Singapore 048763

Printed in the United States of America

*Library of Congress Cataloging-in-Publication Data*

Stebick, Divonna M.
Comprehension strategies for your K–6 literacy classroom: Thinking before, during, and after reading / Divonna M. Stebick and Joy M. Dain.
     p. cm.
Includes bibliographical references and index.
ISBN-13: 978-1-4129-4042-9 (cloth)
ISBN-13: 978-1-4129-4043-6 (pbk.)
   1.  Reading comprehension—Study and teaching (Elementary)
2.  Elementary school teachers—Inservice training. I. Dain, Joy M. II. Title.
LB1573.7.S743 2007
372.47—dc22                                      2006034107

This book is printed on acid-free paper.

07   08   09   10   11   10  9  8  7  6  5  4  3  2  1

| | |
|---|---|
| *Acquisitions Editor:* | Allyson P. Sharp |
| *Editorial Assistant:* | Nadia Kashper |
| *Production Editor:* | Beth A. Bernstein |
| *Copy Editor:* | Gretchen Treadwell |
| *Typesetter:* | C&M Digitals (P) Ltd. |
| *Proofreader:* | Andrea Martin |
| *Indexer:* | Sylvia Coates |
| *Cover Designer:* | Michael Dubowe |
| *Graphic Designer:* | Lisa Riley |
| *Marketing Specialist:* | Maggie Johnson |

# Contents

   *The visual instructional framework of the gradual release
   model integrates current research with authentic examples
   from classroom and text. Application of this framework is
   implemented by the teaching of six comprehension strategies.*

   *Exercising our metacognition increases our ability to think.
   Metacognitive research is supported with authentic classroom
   examples and narratives which encourage readers to gather
   and reorganize their information. Acknowledging the
   interactive model of reading, schema theory is applied to
   the comprehension strategy of making connections.
   Several scripted classroom examples are provided for
   immediate application of making connections using
   the instructional framework.*

   *Demonstrating how questioning provides a multidimensional
   understanding of the text solidifies the other comprehension
   strategies together. Several scripted classroom examples are
   provided for immediate application of questioning using
   the instructional framework.*

# Foreword

From the introductory chapter to the final pages of this user-friendly volume, Divonna Stebick and Joy Dain invite readers to personally engage in a meaningful adventure into classrooms where children actively think. Throughout the journey, teachers are encouraged to negotiate their own thinking, to challenge their developing understandings, and to translate complex comprehension processes into visible and strategic behaviors for their own learners. The authors successfully bring comprehension strategy instruction to life through explicit frameworks for literacy instruction, authentic classroom examples, and high quality instructional resources for K–6 teachers.

Six interrelated chapters provide thorough rationales, demonstrations, and structured plans that will assist novice to expert teachers in charting their own courses with strategy instruction. Specific comprehension strategies are revealed through intriguing classroom scenarios and conscious, sequential instructional procedures that utilize relevant and engaging activities and texts. The chapter formats and presentations also provide thoughtful explanations of how to model specific strategies, design guided practice opportunities, and generate conditions for independent application.

Embedded in the teaching of six comprehension strategies, teachers will navigate through unique instructional activities that translate abstract thought processes into more tangible, concrete concepts. Hands-on activities such as anchor charts, sketches, treasure chests, two-column organizers, and builders' plans are designed to capture students' attention, develop increased awareness of thinking processes, and provide a working knowledge for effective strategy use. These illustrative techniques are anchored by authentic work samples, powerful student examples, and intentional conversations. Quality picture books and expository passages are carefully selected to align with the development of specific comprehension strategies and to match readers' interests and prior knowledge.

Grounded in current theoretical principles, instructional frameworks are described through concrete organizational structures and explicit procedures that systematically transfer ownership of literacy strategies from informed teachers to strategic readers. Consistent before, during, and after reading frameworks are developed for using relevant standards to plan instruction, teacher modeling, guided practice for transferring responsibility to students, and independent application for assuming ownership and self-regulated learning. Active observation, systematic reflection, and precise feedback to cultivate an atmosphere of thinkers are explicitly framed within the context of optimal learning environments.

As evidenced in this innovative text and in their professional lives, Stebick and Dain have displayed sustained enthusiasm and a passionate commitment to enhance and enrich literacy opportunities for all readers. It has been a distinct privilege to examine this enlightening resource and to collaborate with these authors through numerous professional and personal learning experiences. Now, it is my pleasure to invite our readers to proceed forward, to actively think and to reflect, and to energetically continue this journey within their own strategic classrooms.

*—Debra A. Miller*
Associate Professor of Education
McDaniel College
Westminster, Maryland

# Acknowledgments

In appreciation . . .

This book has been the collaborative effort of many people who have passed through our lives over the past several years. Our first thanks go to our most inspirational teachers: Joan Coley, Mary Mann, Barbara Illig-Aviles, and Barbara Stoodt. We would also like to acknowledge our friends and colleagues from Carroll County Public Schools, Gettysburg College, Johns Hopkins University, and McDaniel College. They have laid the foundation for our thinking, dreams, and accomplishments.

Our sincere thanks goes to Crystal Arndt, Audrey Barcroft, Mary Margaret Frederick, Richard Garbutt, Alicia Granger, Carol Grant, Jonathan Hart, Diane Havighurst, Basil Kuzio, Scot Lynn, Mary Mechalske, Andrea Morgan-Littrell, Jenn Myers, Megan Riley, Andrea Smith, Kathy Swaggerty, Jessica Vining, Wendy White, and Gretchen Zimmerman for sharing your energy, insights, reflections, and children as we applied our framework and instructional strategies within your classrooms.

And a special thank you to Jamie Ball, Susan Morgan, and Marcia Talkovich for reviewing our roughest drafts and providing critical feedback. Also, a very special thank you to Debra Miller for the supportive foreword and to Ellin Keene, for sharing your reflective thoughts in our afterword—you inspire us!

The Standards reprinted throughout the book are from *Standards for the English Language Arts* by the International Reading Association and the National Council of Teachers of English, copyright © 1996 by the International Reading Association and the National Council of Teachers of English. Reprinted with permission.

Thank you to the readers in our lives—they showed us what works and what doesn't as we pried into their minds and shared their thinking. They pushed us more than we could have pushed ourselves. When we stepped back to reflect . . . we reflected on you!

Finally, special thanks to Divonna's family: Tim, Jarrod, Jonathan, Grandma, Mom, and Dad, and Joy's family: Gary, Christopher, Patrick,

Mom, and my grandson, Gibson. Your love, laughter, and prayers keep us strong! You mean the world to us!

Corwin Press gratefully acknowledges the contributions of the following reviewers:

Jacie Bejster
Elementary Principal
Crafton Elementary, Carlynton School District
Pittsburgh, PA

Sarah F. Mahurt
Associate Professor
Purdue University
West Lafayette, IN

Richard Marchesani
Assistant Professor of Education
Elmira College
Elmira, NY

Cathy Patterson
Elementary Learning Specialist
Walnut Valley USD
Diamond Bar, CA

Joan Perez, NBCT
Elementary Learning Specialist
Walnut Unified School District
Walnut, CA

Pamela K. Wall
Teacher
Mauldin Elementary School
Simpsonville, SC

# Preface

Most recently, professional development in literacy instruction has become a necessity. We have developed a research-based instructional framework in order to support our nation's pre-service and marginal teachers in grades kindergarten through Grade six to provide explicit comprehension instruction during their language arts classes. Research shows that we are losing many beginning teachers due to lack of professional support. Our text, *Comprehension Strategies for Your K–6 Literacy Classroom: Thinking Before, During, and After Reading,* supports these teachers in a very explicit, research-based manner.

We incorporated Lev Vygotzky's zone of proximal development with David Pearson's gradual release model and Michael Pressley's current comprehension research in order to ensure a strong foundation for our reading comprehension lessons. We consulted the work of other researchers such as Fountas and Pinnell, Duffy, Dole, Farr, Garner, Kucan, Beck, Cooper, Wixson, and Lipson in order to combine theory with field application of six cognitive strategies: activating schema, questioning, visualizing, inferring, determining important ideas, and synthesizing.

Examining each strategy, we tie them directly to the National Council of Teachers of English (NCTE) standards and the International Reading Association (IRA) standards before developing explicit lessons to test in the field. With the current movement toward standard-based education, we align our lessons to NCTE/IRA standards as school systems align their standards to lesson development. The lessons provide the three critical elements necessary for strategic comprehension learning to take place— explicit instruction via teacher modeling, guided practice, and independent application. Each lesson includes the precise language that new and marginal teachers need to articulate for student understanding.

# About the Authors

 **Divonna M. Stebick,** MS Reading, is Instructor of Reading and Language Arts Methods and Assessment at Gettysburg College. She also provides staff development and consultation to school districts and universities. Previously, Divonna spent a number of years in the Carroll County Public School System in Carroll County, Maryland. She served as a classroom teacher and an Integrated Language Arts Specialist/Staff Developer. Contact information is available at her web site: http://www.divonna stebick.com.

 **Joy M. Dain,** MS Reading, is Coordinator of Staff Development for the Carroll County Public School System and an adjunct at McDaniel College. Joy's 22 years in education include working as a classroom teacher, a reading specialist, and a staff developer in various school systems.

# Introduction

As educators, we seem to have more questions than answers to the complexity of reading. It seems that the more we read, the more we learn; the more we learn, the more we question. Will our prior knowledge interfere or enhance comprehending? What specific words will lift off the page and interact with our experiences? How and when do we maneuver independently through the text? Does this ever happen or do we rely on family, friends, teachers, or colleagues to help us gain or maintain control? Does comprehending look or sound differently to our spouses, our children, our own classroom of students, our friends, and fellow educators? How much support will our students need to understand the concept of comprehension behaviors? How much support will our students need to understand a text or a topic? As teachers, we often address these questions, but somehow, we know the variables that interplay with the reading process outweigh the answers. Posing these questions to colleagues, observing classrooms, and listening to conversations between teacher and student led us to writing this book.

As literacy staff developers in regional education centers (Regional education centers are comprehensive schools that provide services with regular, academically challenged, behaviorally challenged, emotionally challenged, and ELL students. The diversity in each classroom continuously challenges the regular and special educators as they collaborate to meet the needs of their learners.), these questions were paramount in our day-to-day interactions with faculty and students. We believe the essence of high quality teaching is collaboration, and we have developed processes to share our expertise in order to negotiate meaning and learning for both teacher and student. We know we need to develop thinkers who can construct meaning.

Realizing our literacy staff development positions could be a critical part of the grand dilemma, we reflected: How do we support our teachers to meet the needs of their diverse learners? Sharing our reflective thoughts with colleagues, it became evident that their concerns were even deeper;

how does the gradual release model work in a standards-driven culture? How can I make comprehension instruction come alive? Where do I begin?

## HOW DOES THE GRADUAL RELEASE MODEL WORK IN A STANDARDS-DRIVEN CULTURE?

As Kucan and Beck (1997) suggest, struggling readers thrive in an explicit instructional environment, since implicit instruction is contingent upon readers who are already able to engage actively in the process. Passive readers do not have the necessary tools for unlocking texts, and because of this they need multiple reading comprehension strategies. Research is replete with examples of the importance of organized instruction to benefit all readers, including those proficient and less proficient.

Writers consider their audience. Reading teachers consider their audiences' experiences, the structure and features of texts, and the context in which the information will be learned. We use texts to model comprehension strategies, provide guided practice, and offer opportunities for independent application. Our Before, During, and After (BDA) Instructional Framework is based on this premise.

In a developmentally appropriate way, teachers should explicitly describe each cognitive strategy, model the strategy, allow guided practice time, and release the students in an optimal learning environment to apply this learned strategy independently (Zemelman, Daniels, & Hyde, 2005). This combination of explicit teaching and gradual transfer of responsibility from teacher to student is especially critical for struggling readers (Routman, 2003). The teacher provides explicit instruction during the modeling phase. Over the course of several days, the teacher scaffolds the student's thinking through Think Alouds and during guided practice. Finally, the student needs opportunities to practice and apply the learned strategy during independent application.

Within our BDA framework, modeling begins before we even step in front of the students. We consider the students' prior knowledge at the literal and world levels and how to connect the strategy to the students' known experiences (Vygotzky, 1978). At this point, most of the responsibility is the teacher's. Once the students can make the connection, we are able to acknowledge a balance of ownership of strategy and mental processing by providing supports through explicit teaching. Careful monitoring and transfer of language throughout the gradual release model allow for the ownership to transfer to the student. The instruction begins when the teacher chooses material for teaching purposes; the explicit instruction is teacher regulated in the I Do phase. During this phase the teacher independently models the strategy expectations as students do not interfere with

**Table I.1**

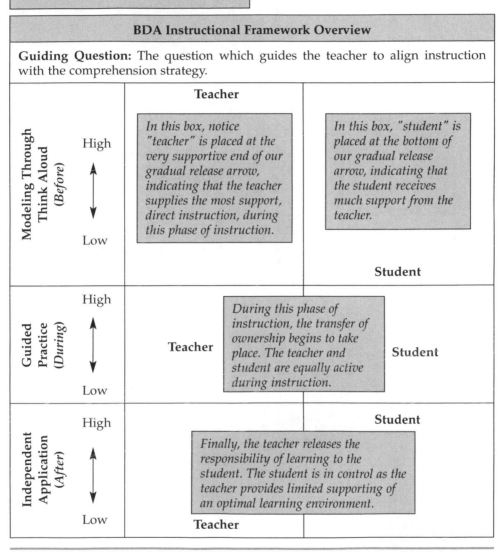

Our arrow in the left column is an iconic reminder of the gradual release model. The level of teacher and student interaction is indicated by the placement of the watermarks in the next two columns.

**BDA Instructional Framework Overview**

**Guiding Question:** The question which guides the teacher to align instruction with the comprehension strategy.

|  |  | **Teacher** | |
|---|---|---|---|
| **Modeling Through Think Aloud** *(Before)* | High ↕ Low | In this box, notice "teacher" is placed at the very supportive end of our gradual release arrow, indicating that the teacher supplies the most support, direct instruction, during this phase of instruction. | In this box, "student" is placed at the bottom of our gradual release arrow, indicating that the student receives much support from the teacher. |
|  |  |  | **Student** |
| **Guided Practice** *(During)* | High ↕ Low | **Teacher** During this phase of instruction, the transfer of ownership begins to take place. The teacher and student are equally active during instruction. | **Student** |
|  |  |  | **Student** |
| **Independent Application** *(After)* | High ↕ Low | Finally, the teacher releases the responsibility of learning to the student. The student is in control as the teacher provides limited supporting of an optimal learning environment. **Teacher** |  |

the teacher's Think Aloud. As the students demonstrate some competency, the reading material is negotiated and matched to the students' needs, while the teacher scaffolds the students' learning in the We Do phase. Students now begin to actively participate in the Think Aloud. Finally, the students regulate their learning as they choose their material during the You Do phase (Wilhelm, 2001b).

**Table I.2**

HIGH ←————→ LOW

| Gradual Release Model | I DO<br>*Teacher* | WE DO<br>*Teacher and Student* | YOU DO<br>*Student* |
|---|---|---|---|
| Think Aloud<br><br>**BEFORE** | • Assess students' strengths and needs<br>• Provide explicit instruction through modeling | • Share reflections on thinking process | • Student observes modeling |
| Guided Reading<br><br>**DURING** | • Assess students' strengths and needs<br>• Plan appropriate text introduction<br>• Introduce text<br>• Teacher makes observational notes | • Teacher provides supportive text processing strategies<br>• Teacher provides supportive text comprehending behaviors<br>• Student reads and processes text<br>• Teacher makes observational notes | • Student applies text processing strategies while reading selected text<br>• Student applies comprehending behaviors while reading selected text |
| Independent Reading<br><br>**INDEPENDENT APPLICATION** | • Teacher confers with students<br>• Teacher provides specific language to support learner needs<br>• Names and identifies student behaviors | • Student asks questions<br>• Student demonstrates ability to apply text processing strategies<br>• Student demonstrates ability to apply comprehending behaviors<br>• Teacher makes observational notes | • Student applies text processing strategies while reading self-selected text<br>• Student applies comprehending behaviors while reading self-selected text<br>• Student reflects on his/her understanding |

HIGH ←————→ LOW

Visually, our BDA framework provides a structure for transferring ownership to the students. Theoretically, the framework provides the lenses to clarify the process and strategies for reading and writing. Our BDA framework allows teachers to validate clear learning goals by defining the guiding questions during each part of the reading and writing lesson. It also provides a place to identify and record student learning goals, where reflection can evolve after a lesson is taught. Reflecting upon each part of the lesson, we're able to monitor our students' progress based on these goals. Feedback is essential, yet easy to gather during the after section of the lesson.

In the second BDA framework, the instructional responsibility lies upon the teacher while the accountability for active listening lies upon the student. Remember, modeling for any specific strategy may continue throughout the course of the year. This depends upon the needs of the students. During guided practice, the teacher scaffolds the thinking for the group, allowing the students to negotiate through the text with some success of application. This is crucial for students to see the connection between direct instruction and application. Not only do students need to see it, but they also need to hear the same verbiage in different settings. Observing during guided practice will verify the amount of modeling students will need for continued support. Guided practice also needs to happen over the course of several days, using appropriate texts. These texts may be picture books, basal reader selections, or little readers used in guided reading instruction that lend themselves to making connections. Opportunities for independent practice are critical for all students to succeed as thinkers. Independent practice is more than sustained silent reading—it is an activity that gives students a substantial amount of time in an optimal learning environment to apply what was learned. Teachers create this optimal learning environment by carefully monitoring each student's reading behaviors through individual conferences. The students then apply what they learned by accessing instructionally appropriate materials. These materials allow for opportunities to demonstrate the specific learned comprehension strategies.

The students' endurance is slowly built. In September, we start with ten minutes of silent reading and we add minutes to each week, working the group up to 20 active minutes of independent reading time. As the students read, we monitor their behaviors while taking judicious notes. We question the students regarding their selections; we note those that followed procedures, and the students who are able to apply the specific strategy. As always, we constantly ask ourselves:

- What did I learn about my students?
- What did I learn about my teaching?

By answering these two questions, we know the impact of the gradual release of responsibility will be reconfigured to meet the needs of the students. Differentiating instruction provides the support for student learning.

## HOW CAN I MAKE COMPREHENSION INSTRUCTION COME ALIVE?

We need to think about our thinking (Flavell, 1979). Thoughtful readers develop, implement, and adjust their plans as they read.

As adult readers, we try to avoid those authors where little thinking is needed. The words are superficial. The character names change but the story structure remains the same. Hopefully, we can select books where the words become embedded in our own life experiences. We consciously or unconsciously monitor our application of reading strategies to provide an understanding. Reading Anna Quindlen's *A Short Guide to a Happy Life*, *Black and Blue*, or *Blessings*, we purposefully notice how and why we reread a passage, when we create a picture in our heads, and when questions and predictions abound throughout. Her descriptions and her use of a simple word like "rattled" in the book *Blessings* describe how Lydia Blessings, in her later life, felt visiting the cemetery. "The cemetery rattled her more than she would have expected" (2002, pp. 93–94).

This simple word creates an image not only in our heads, but in our hearts too. The responsibility of comprehension rests upon the interaction between the reader and the author's words:

At least she had a cradle now, a carved cherry cradle on shallow rockers that Mrs. Blessing had told him to come and take from a musty back bedroom in the big house. He had tickled himself with the thought of tying a string to his toe and looping its other end around the ornamental curves at the head of the little bed so that in the nighttime he could rock her without getting up. But she was such a good baby now, so orderly and cooperative in her habits that the idea was more of a cartoon construct than anything he heeded to consider. He felt stupid sometimes, how he liked to watch her, how he still flinched when she popped herself in the nose with her spastic fist, how her face went real still and her mouth opened as she watched the sunlight shoot down onto the floor next to her blanket, how she would smile like a spasm and it would go straight to his heart. (2002, pp. 93–94)

As you read this passage:

- Did any words create a clear picture in your head?
- Did the words conjure a smell only newborns have in your memory?
- Were those images tied to your prior experiences?
- How many words were absorbed before comprehension began?
- When did you stop comprehending?
- Did the words remain one-dimensional because of your experiences or interest?

For those of us who are mothers or caretakers, or have witnessed the "spastic" movements of newborns, comprehension begins immediately. Variations depend upon our age, our experiences, and the relationships we have with family and friends.

## WHERE DO I BEGIN?

Throughout this book, you will read about many reading and writing experiences of teachers and students; we invite you to be the reader and writer.

Take some time now to practice another reading strategy—rereading. Reread this excerpt from Anna Quindlen's *Blessings*. As you reread, please record your thoughts in the space provided.

**Table I.3**

| As a reader, I thought . . . | As a writer, I thought . . . |
|---|---|
|  |  |

At least she had a cradle now, a carved cherry cradle on shallow rockers that Mrs. Blessing had told him to come and take from a musty back bedroom in the big house. He had tickled himself with the thought of tying a string to his toe and looping its other end around the ornamental curves at the head of the little bed so that in the nighttime he could rock her without getting up. But she was such a good baby now, so orderly and cooperative in her habits that the idea was more of a cartoon construct than anything he heeded to consider. He felt stupid sometimes, how he liked to watch her, how he still flinched when she popped herself in the nose with her spastic fist, how her face went real still and her mouth opened as she watched the sunlight shoot down onto the floor next to her blanket, how she would smile like a spasm and it would go straight to his heart. (2002, pp. 93–94)

Now, review what you thought as you read. Just as good readers visualize as a reader, authors visualize too. Writers make natural connections to their own experiences and selectively choose words to create a picture in the readers' minds. Authors remember to include only the most critical information and details.

We have developed a framework to assist instructional planning in order to meet the readers' and writers' needs congruently. Before you begin your journey through the rest of our book, please take some time to reply to our guiding question; describe what reading looks like in each instructional phase for the teacher and the student.

You will have an opportunity to reply to other reflective questions after each chapter.

We know instruction needs to emphasize connections between reading and writing. We need to develop students' abilities to write like a reader and read like a writer (Pearson, 2002). If we want students to write in a variety of genres, then we need them to be able to comprehend this variety of genres.

## HOW DO I MEET THE NEEDS OF OUR STANDARDS-DRIVEN CULTURE?

The six chapters focus on six comprehension strategies. Each strategy is developed by four BDA frameworks. To meet the needs of our standards-driven culture, our first framework provides an overview of the highlighted comprehension strategy and connects to the National Council of Teachers of English (NCTE) standards because standards vary at the state

**Table I.4**

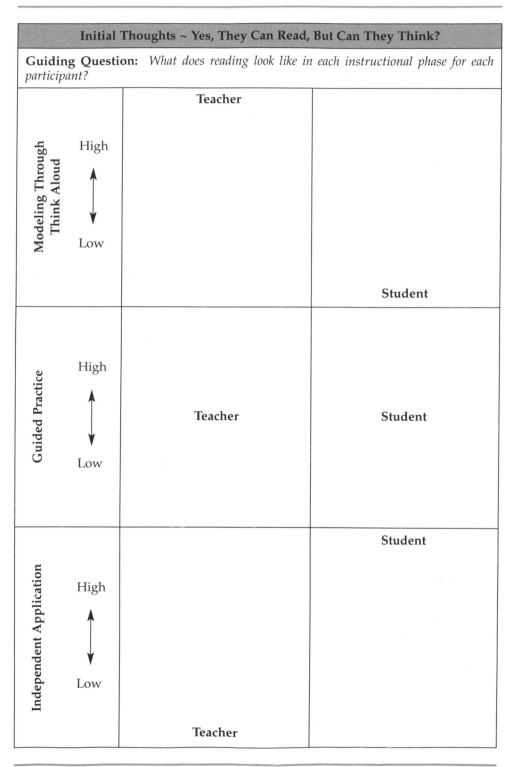

| Initial Thoughts ~ Yes, They Can Read, But Can They Think? | | |
|---|---|---|

**Guiding Question:** *What does reading look like in each instructional phase for each participant?*

level. In the subsequent frameworks, the interaction between the teacher and the student is based upon the application of the gradual release model. Explicit teaching is shared through teacher talk and modeling examples in the second framework. During guided practice, the transfer of responsibility begins to unfold in the third framework, and examples of guided practice and scaffolding are shared. Finally, the students take ownership in the fourth framework as they independently apply the strategies.

Chapter 1 provides the foundation for making meaning—schema development. We address how to assess and develop prior knowledge. We exercise students' metacognition in order to improve their ability to think. Using the interactive model of reading, we apply schema theory to the comprehension strategy of making connections.

Chapter 2 demonstrates how questioning provides a multidimensional understanding of the text and solidifies the other comprehension strategies together. We script various lessons using fictional picture books to model.

Chapter 3 reveals the interrelationships between text and the reader's personal experiences. We also capture how these private relationships enhance the reader's understanding by tapping into the reader's five senses as they visualize.

In Chapter 4 we address the most intrinsic comprehension behavior—inferring. We exhibit the interrelationships between comprehending illustrations and/or comprehending text to construct personal interpretations of the text. We provide sequential, fictional picture book lessons allowing the reader to watch as we scaffold student learning using the gradual release model of instruction.

Chapter 5 takes us into nonfiction texts, as we show how to make these texts accessible for all learners. We also focus on the need to generate a thinking question using the text's format, features, content, and/or the student's personal curiosity to refine details or facts as readers construct meaning in order to determine what is most important.

In Chapter 6, we synthesize students' thinking by explaining the integration of questioning, determining important ideas, and the readers' prior knowledge to create an original idea, see a new perspective, or form a new line of thinking.

Provided in the resource section are templates capturing our BDA framework, strategy organizers, and other instructional planning tools you may reproduce for your classroom needs. We have also identified texts we recommend for teaching each of the comprehension strategies.

Realizing the importance of metacognitive behaviors, we address the function and purpose throughout each of our comprehension chapters. In addition, we breathe life into each of the comprehension strategies; we provide a concrete example for each of the abstract thinking processes of reading. We make the invisible visible.

# **1** Reorganizing Our Thinking

*Making Connections*

*The illiterate of the twenty-first century will not be those who cannot read and write, but those who cannot learn, unlearn, and relearn.*

—Alvin Toffler

Remembering my first read of *Thank You, Mr. Falker,* by Patricia Polacco (1998), I immediately think of Mr. Dion, my fifth grade teacher at Prospect Elementary School in East Cleveland, Ohio. He taught us "arithmetic" by filling out purchase orders for the school store; he taught us how to average numbers by having us add up our grades in science and social studies, and then divide by the number of tests. He taught us to read not only by Scott Foresman's *The New Frontier* series, but also by going to the library and self-selecting books to read. Just as Mr. Dion was an anomaly in 1960, so is Mr. Falker in Polacco's book. Both care about their students and both certainly have some unconventional methods for helping students believe in themselves as readers, writers, and thinkers.

Since my schema brought me back to Mr. Dion's classroom, Polacco's words have a much richer meaning for me than they do for Mary Mechalske's fourth grade inclusion students. To enhance and enrich their understanding, I share my personal experiences with Mr. Dion and proceed to share Polacco's book . . .

Trisha's grandma used to say that the stars were holes in the sky. They were the light of heaven coming from the other side. And she used to say that someday she would be on the other side, where the light comes from.

But it was not long after that night that her grandma must have let go of the grass, because she went to where the lights were, on the other side. And not long after that, Trisha's grandpa let go of the grass, too. (1998, p. 9)

The expectation in Mary's classroom is for her students to listen to a picture book from her Treasure Chest at least three times. (Treasure Chest books are those texts that can be revisited multiple times for strategy instruction, allow for a multitude of discussion, and have some connections to the students' prior knowledge.) The first time is for listening for the global understanding (Langer, 1995). The second time is for explicit instruction—the I Do phase for comprehension strategy instruction.

Entering Mary's room, I listen to her rereading of *An Angel for Solomon Singer,* by Cynthia Rylant (1996). Mary stops periodically and thinks aloud about her questions. She continues this process until she models a variety of questions. In order to engage her students without compromising her opportunities for exemplary models, Mary allows her students to write down their questions. Mary then begins to transfer the ownership over to her students. This transfer of ownership relies on Mary's ability to pre-assess her students' prior knowledge and observe their interactions with texts. Mary uses Wiggins and McTighe's backward design model to achieve these planning goals where standards and learning goals are identified first, assessments are developed next, and instructional activities are planned to support the standards and assessments (2005). Mary continuously takes notes on how students apply what they have learned in previous lessons with what they have experienced in their personal lives; this allows her to determine where her direct instruction begins, the level of scaffolding needed during guided practice, and how to create an optimal learning environment for students to independently apply these strategies. (An optimal learning environment includes materials and strategies to match the specific learners' needs.)

By watching and listening to Mary, one can see that her students have an understanding of the process thanks to her explicit teaching. Now, the students' main focus can be upon the strategy itself. Mary has her students share their questions, asking if they think their questions will be answered from the book or from their prior knowledge. Once again, she models strategic ownership.

# ACTIVATING PRIOR KNOWLEDGE

It was six years ago when I first entered Mary's fourth grade classroom. As soon as I crossed the threshold, an old, harvest gold chair caught my eye. This chair is still the focal point for learning. Mary positions her students on the carpet and at nearby desks. With students strategically located in a small area, conversations and learning can naturally happen. In addition, markers, wipe boards, clipboards, pencils, and large chart paper are readily available. Displayed are the many anchor charts the students have developed together. (According to Harvey and Goudvis [2002], anchor charts can record students' thinking about a text, lesson, or strategy so that we can return to it to remember the process. Anchor charts connect past teaching and learning to future teaching and learning. Everyone weighs in to construct meaning and hold thinking.) Mary has created an environment for literacy learning.

Approaching the harvest gold chair with my overstuffed Barbie suitcase, the students begin to laugh. With the bulging case expanding the zipper teeth, I plop myself into the chair and exclaim, "My bags are packed!"

Arousing their curiosity, they immediately want to know what is inside. Before opening the suitcase, I share our destination. "We are headed to an island for fun and relaxation." Before we begin, I tell the students there are too many items. In fact, there are some items we don't even need. We need to decide what we can leave behind and what we will need to include on our trip.

Unzipping the suitcase, the top pops open and some of the items begin to hang over the side. Pulling out a swimsuit, I ask if we need to keep this item. All of the children's heads nod up and down in agreement. Next I pull out some suntan lotion and a magazine. Again they all agree. Pulling out a scarf and a pair of mittens, the group yells in unison, "No way!" This time I reach in and pull out airplane tickets, a camera, a towel, pair of shorts, and a pair of woolen socks. Each time I pull an item out of the suitcase, I ask for confirmation of their answer. Each student justifies his or her answer by using prior knowledge about islands, understanding of climate, and experiences of vacationing at Ocean City, Maryland.

Looking at our pile, I ask the students, "How should we repack our suitcase? What items do we want on the bottom? Do you want specific items on top? Or do we just throw all the needed things back into the suitcase? And what do we do with the scarf, mittens, woolen socks, heavy sweater, and boots?" One student suggests we leave the scarf, mittens, and other unnecessary items on the floor.

She says, "That's what I do at home." For packing, another friend states we should just throw the items into the suitcase and another student disagrees, but each validates his or her reasons. The first student says it doesn't matter what order the suitcase is packed because we can just dump everything out.

The other friend says, "One time my family's luggage was lost by the airline. If we hadn't put our bathing suits in our carry-on with another set of clothes, we would have had to go out and buy something or wait till the airline found our luggage. And that wouldn't have been fun."

Continuing on this journey, I proceed to share with them how preparing for a trip is like reading for understanding. You need to know your destination, what kinds of equipment you may need for a successful trip, and if you have to make any adjustments for missing items such as a bathing suit. Active readers do the same thing. They develop a plan for reading and set a specific purpose. They decide which strategies they may need to comprehend and if their comprehension breaks down, what adjustments they will need to make.

## Metacognition

Going through this simple exercise of noticing, selecting and reorganizing items in the suitcase provides an anchor for metacognitive behaviors. The exercise transforms the abstract process of metacognition into concrete terms for students. Creating the strategic reading behaviors into concrete ideas will help develop an understanding of the cognitive processes of reading (Pressley, Borkowski, & Schneider, 1987). As Garner (1988) found, metacognition (thinking about one's thinking) has been found to be a critical skill requiring teachers to intentionally model (According to Knuth and Jones [1991], modeling is showing a student how to complete a task with the expectation that the student will then emulate the model. In reading, modeling often involves talking about how one thinks through a task.), to show rather than tell, and to scaffold (providing teacher support to students by modeling the thought processes in a learning episode and gradually shifting the responsibility for formulating questions and thinking aloud to the students [Knuth & Jones, 1991]) rather than expect that students develop these literacy strategies on their own. Another important consideration found in Garner's literature is a teacher's ability to recognize how and when to implement cognitive strategies (mental operations to assist learning) while reading to make meaning.

Metacognition is knowledge about the processes that helps the reader successfully navigate through text. In addition, it is also knowing when, why, and how to activate text processing or comprehending strategies (Ruetzel, Camperell, & Smith, 2002). It is self-knowledge or the understanding of one's capacity of comprehending. For example, when reading unfamiliar material, I need a quiet area with no outside distractions. I use a pencil for underlining and taking notes. If comprehension breaks down, I automatically self-question for clarification and make adjustments to help infuse the author's intent with intent for learning a specific idea, concept, or thought (Brown, Armbruster, & Baker, 1986; Flavell, 1979).

Consequently, three years later, I continue the same initial procedures with the suitcase, but this time in Wendy's fourth grade classroom. Having a better understanding of the metacognitive processing, I realize strategic instruction (which includes analyzing the student needs, establishing rationale for the lesson, and assessing the lesson outcome to determine the next steps) needs to be continuous. As before, I begin with "thinking about our thinking" (Flavell, 1979).

## Day One

Tucked under my arm are several books and a Peanuts cartoon to begin the day's lesson. I decide to put the overhead on the floor and have the children gather around. Projecting the Peanuts cartoon on the lower wall, the students notice Peppermint Patty sucked inside the couch with a frazzled look on her face.

Turning back to the students, both Wendy and I share how these same behaviors happen to adults too. As we each provide an example from our own literate lives, one student says, "I can't believe you two didn't know what you were reading!" The students begin to share their own experiences.

Jacob starts with an example from last school year. "I was reading something in science class about flight and I didn't understand how the plane's wings moved up and down."

Raising her hand, Christina shares her experiences with reading at home. Before long, we have many examples charted on the overhead. Moving to the chart paper, I proceed to write the word "metacognition" on top of the chart. As I write, I hear students whisper "meta" under their breath. Looking at the students' faces, I complete the word for them and ask them to read the word with me.

Heading toward the suitcase, I roll it closer to the chart and begin to share how yesterday's lesson connects to our understanding of metacognition. As readers, we need to know our destination, or what kind of text we will be reading. We need to know what comprehensive strategies we will need to be an active reader, or what kinds of clothes to pack. We need to recognize when comprehension breaks down and know how to make adjustments, or recognize when we need to reorganize our clothing and other items for our trip. Yesterday, we questioned ourselves as we repacked our suitcase. As readers, we do the same thing. Self-questioning is the tool which helps us repack and/or reorganize our thinking before, during, or after reading (Reutzel, Camperell, & Smith, 2002). Finishing for the day, we add the words "thinking about your thinking" and "self-questioning" to our metacognition anchor chart.

Planning for the next day, Wendy and I decide upon the text, *Hey, Little Ant* by Phillip and Hannah Hoose. The layout of the text is organized as scripted dialogue between two characters in the story, the child and the ant. The child wants to squish the ant but the ant pleads to the child. The ant wants the child to see how they are alike. At the end of the text, the authors reverse roles between the ant and the child.

The authors pose the question from the ant's point of view, "If you were me and I were you, what would you want me to do?" On the very last page, the illustrator continues the scenario by drawing a huge shoe with the ant carrying two suitcases and standing in the shoe's shadow. The authors continue asking the reader questions, "Should the ant get squished? Should the ant go free?"

The text provides many opportunities for questioning and predicting, and for thinking metacognitively about the text layout, the authors' style and intent, and how all of these attributes can alter meaning through self-questioning.

## Day Two

Waiting for my arrival, Wendy begins reviewing the previous day's lessons by asking her students several clarifying questions:

- As a reader, how do you know when you are having difficulty understanding the text?
- How do you know you comprehend the text?
- Why would self-questioning be a good technique to use?

As expected, the students have difficulty articulating their ideas but they understand it is okay to be reading the words yet not comprehending the meaning. If comprehension breaks down or their understanding fades as they are reading, they understand the importance of stopping and self-questioning to clarify.

After the students finish sharing, I begin my Think Aloud. Borrowing from *Reading With Meaning* by Debbie Miller (2002), I tell the students that when they see me put the book on my lap, I will be sharing my thinking—or my self-talking. One little girl raises her hand and says, "That's okay Mrs. Dain, my mom talks to herself all the time."

Reading the title and looking at the front cover, I begin to model my self-talk about the type of text and what expectations I have for the story frame. Opening the book, reading the first two pages, and noticing the scripted dialogue, I begin to tell them how I have changed my plan, or reorganized my suitcase. I now need to think about reading the text as a conversation between the child and the ant. Continuing through the book, I specifically point out how the authors have developed a sense of empathy for the ant by having the story told from the ant's point of view. I also share with them a couple of questions that keep popping up as I read, and how the questions help me develop a deeper understanding of the story. I decide to quickly revisit the text, stopping where I self-talked my way through. Charting my thinking, I share with the students how and where I stop to reorganize and repack my understanding.

After the students leave, Wendy and I talk about the importance of continuing the processes of explicitly teaching metacognition and keeping up with the anchor charts. Sitting down with *Strategies That Work,* we find in chapter two the research from Perkins and Swartz and definitions for four developmental levels of metacognitive knowledge. They reference "tacit learners" who lack awareness of what is inside their suitcase. "Aware learners" know their destination but make no adjustments for their trip. "Strategic learners" are able to repack or reorganize their suitcase and "reflective learners" can repack, reorganize, and reflect upon their decisions for a successful trip. Knowing that our goal for the school year is to help Wendy's students be strategic and reflective readers, we decide to continue sharing our thinking during shared reading and guided reading. More important, after independent reading we specifically ask students what comprehending behaviors they initiated and how they used them. Students need to hear us and see us apply the language of a reader. We must show our students how we think while we read (Wilhelm, 2001a). Asking them to articulate their understanding of the language and processes helps them become strategic, reflective readers.

## Developing Schema

In our experiences, we relate schema theory to a personal, mental file cabinet (Armbruster & Anderson, 1984). Schematically, we see how the student readers have cross-categorized their worldly experiences, how they have organized their understanding of text factors, and how they have stored their learning behaviors. Good readers organize their prior knowledge into these three interconnected systems.

Reading is seen as an active process of constructing meaning by connecting old knowledge with newly encountered information in text (Dole, Duffy, Roehler, & Pearson, 1991). When we select an appropriate text to model connections, we are aware of the student's prior knowledge. If time is not well spent matching text to student's prior knowledge then the student won't be able to activate his/her schemata to comprehend.

In order to be successful with comprehending we need to be cognizant of these three factors: the reader, the text, and the context (Lipson & Wixson, 2003). A skilled teacher pays attention to the reader's prior knowledge, where and when the strategy instruction will be modeled, and the type of text or texts to use.

In Table 1.1 on the next page, we can visually see the responsibility of the student and the teacher for each of the schema lessons and the setting where the strategy instruction occurs. In Kathy Swaggerty's fourth grade classroom, I specifically selected text that connected to the students' worldly knowledge.

After the teacher analyzes the students' prior knowledge, she is prepared to activate their schemata. In order to develop the mental framework, students need to understand the text. The teacher begins to explicitly teach by modeling her thinking (see Table 1.2).

After the teacher feels she has shared enough exemplary models of her thinking, she begins to release the responsibility of learning to her students. She invites them to share their connections (see Table 1.3).

Once again, the teacher analyzes the students' learning. She creates an optimal learning environment for them to apply what they learned. She selects texts at the students' independent instructional levels that offer opportunities for making connections to develop their schemata. According to Fountas and Pinnell (2001) it is critical to carefully select these texts in order to truly engage the readers (see Table 1.4).

*(Text Continues on Page 28)*

**Table 1.1**

| NCTE Standards: |
| --- |
| 1.   Students read a wide range of print and nonprint texts to build an understanding of texts, of themselves, and of the cultures of the United States and the world; to acquire new information; to respond to the needs and demands of society and the workplace; and for personal fulfillment. Among these texts are fiction and nonfiction, classic and contemporary works.<br><br>3.   Students apply a wide range of strategies to comprehend, interpret, evaluate, and appreciate texts. They draw on their prior experience, their interactions with other readers and writers, their knowledge of word meaning and of other texts, their word identification strategies, and their understanding of textual features (e.g., sound-letter correspondence, sentence structure, context, graphics). |

| Guiding Question: *How will students be able to draw upon prior experiences to enhance their understanding?* | | |
| --- | --- | --- |
| **Modeling Through Think Aloud** High ↕ Low | **Teacher**<br>Build an understanding of text and the interrelationships of the reader and the author by drawing upon students' prior experiences. | Develops an awareness of activating prior knowledge.<br><br>**Student** |
| **Guided Practice** High ↕ Low | Continue to build an understanding of text and the interrelationships of the reader and the author by drawing upon students' prior experiences.<br><br>**Teacher** | Begins to activate prior knowledge to build an understanding of text.<br><br>**Student** |
| **Independent Application** High ↕ Low | Monitor students' activation of prior knowledge and understanding of text.<br><br>**Teacher** | **Student**<br>Builds an understanding of text and the interrelationships of the reader and the author by drawing upon prior experiences. |

**Table 1.2** BDA for Teacher Modeling Schemata

**NCTE Standards:**

**1.** Students read a wide range of print and nonprint texts to build an understanding of texts, of themselves, and of the cultures of the United States and the world; to acquire new information; to respond to the needs and demands of society and the workplace; and for personal fulfillment. Among these texts are fiction and nonfiction, classic and contemporary works.

**3.** Students apply a wide range of strategies to comprehend, interpret, evaluate, and appreciate texts. They draw on their prior experience, their interactions with other readers and writers, their knowledge of word meaning and of other texts, their word identification strategies, and their understanding of textual features (e.g., sound-letter correspondence, sentence structure, context, graphics).

**Picture Book:** *Thank You, Mr. Falker* by Patricia Polacco

| Before (High ↕ Low) | **Teacher** | |
|---|---|---|
| | *Let's look at this front cover. As a reader what do we notice?* | *I notice two kids and a teacher.* |
| | *Who do you think the teacher is?* | *Mr. Falker* |
| | *Remember we learn about characters by what they say, how they interact with other characters and what they do. Notice the character's facial expressions. Do you think there may be a problem?* | *The little girl is having trouble with reading or writing.* |
| | *Let's look at Mr. Falker's eyes. What do you think he might be thinking?* | |
| | *So far, we've established who some of the characters are. We know that there is a problem. Where do you think the setting might take place?* | *In school* |
| | *How will Mr. Falker help the characters in the story?* | |
| | *Will he react differently to different characters?* | **Student** |

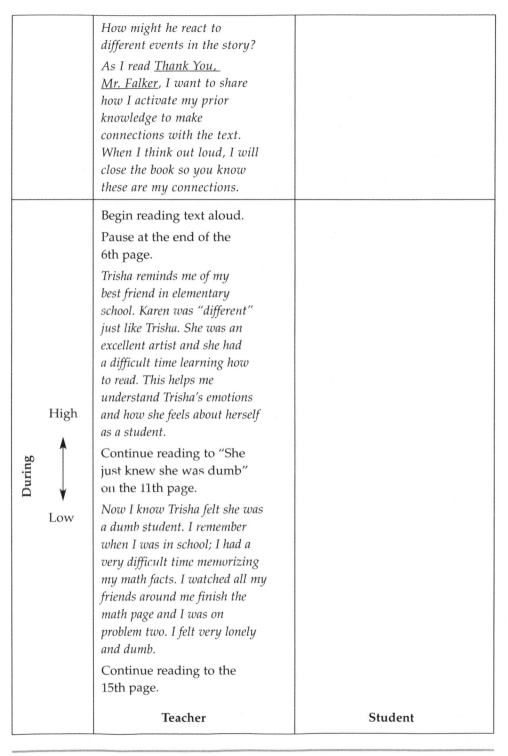

| | Teacher | Student |
|---|---|---|
| | *How might he react to different events in the story?*<br><br>*As I read* <u>Thank You, Mr. Falker</u>, *I want to share how I activate my prior knowledge to make connections with the text. When I think out loud, I will close the book so you know these are my connections.* | |
| **During**<br>High ↕ Low | Begin reading text aloud.<br><br>Pause at the end of the 6th page.<br><br>*Trisha reminds me of my best friend in elementary school. Karen was "different" just like Trisha. She was an excellent artist and she had a difficult time learning how to read. This helps me understand Trisha's emotions and how she feels about herself as a student.*<br><br>Continue reading to "She just knew she was dumb" on the 11th page.<br><br>*Now I know Trisha felt she was a dumb student. I remember when I was in school; I had a very difficult time memorizing my math facts. I watched all my friends around me finish the math page and I was on problem two. I felt very lonely and dumb.*<br><br>Continue reading to the 15th page. | |

*(Continued)*

**Table 1.2** (Continued)

| | | |
|---|---|---|
| | *Wow! Even though Trisha moved to a different state, her problems still continue. This reminds me of my last day of third grade. I thought I would never see a math fact quiz again! Then on the first day of fourth grade, my teacher gave the class a timed math fact sheet. Just like Trisha's classmates called her a baby, my friends made fun of me too. I was thinking like Trisha. I wanted to roll up into a little ball and hide.* | |
| | Continue to the end of the 17th page. | |
| | *Mr. Falker reminds me of my fifth grade teacher, Mr. Dion. He was the only male teacher I ever had in elementary school and instead of a necktie; he always wore a bow tie. Just like Mr. Falker, Mr. Dion had no favorites! By looking at Trisha's facial expressions, I think she has a feeling of hope that this year will be different, just like I did when I met Mr. Dion.* | |
| | Continue to read to the 27th page. | |
| | *This reminds me of how Mr. Dion taught differently. He taught us arithmetic by filling out purchase orders for the school store, he taught us the meaning of how to average numbers by having us add up our grades in science and* | |

| | | | |
|---|---|---|---|
| | | *social studies and then dividing by the number of tests. All of a sudden he brought learning to life.* <br><br> Continue reading the rest of the book. <br><br> *I learned to love school the same year as Trisha, because of our fifth grade teachers.* | |
| **After** | High ↑↓ Low | *As we look back at my T-Chart we can see I used my prior knowledge to build an understanding of* <u>Thank You, Mr. Falker.</u> <br><br> **Teacher** | **Student** |

**Table 1.3**   BDA for Guided Practice Using Schemata

---

**NCTE Standards:**

**1.** Students read a wide range of print and nonprint texts to build an understanding of texts, of themselves, and of the cultures of the United States and the world; to acquire new information; to respond to the needs and demands of society and the workplace; and for personal fulfillment. Among these texts are fiction and nonfiction, classic and contemporary works.

**3.** Students apply a wide range of strategies to comprehend, interpret, evaluate, and appreciate texts. They draw on their prior experience, their interactions with other readers and writers, their knowledge of word meaning and of other texts, their word identification strategies, and their understanding of textual features (e.g., sound-letter correspondence, sentence structure, context, graphics).

**Picture Book:** *Thank You, Mr. Falker* by Patricia Polacco

---

*(Continued)*

**Table 1.3** (Continued)

| | | **Teacher** | |
|---|---|---|---|
| **Before** | High ↕ Low | *Remember when I read* <u>Thank You, Mr. Falker</u> *and I almost became Trisha. By using my prior knowledge, it helped me have a better understanding of the character and the problem.*<br><br>*You will have an opportunity } to read _____ and place yourself in the text. You will use your prior knowledge to make connections as you build your understanding. This T-Chart will help you organize and connect your thoughts. On the left side of the chart, write the author's words and on the side next to the author's words write down your prior knowledge and how it helped you understand the text.* | **Student** |
| **During** | High ↕ Low | Monitor students' reading behaviors and scaffold their use of prior knowledge. Make sure prior knowledge is appropriate and connections enhance their understanding. Provide specific examples when this process breaks down.<br><br>**Teacher** | Read _____ and record thoughts and connections.<br><br><br><br><br>**Student** |
| **After** | High ↕ Low | Ask for student volunteers to share their T-Charts and share how their prior knowledge developed their understanding.<br><br>**Teacher** | **Student**<br>Share T-Charts. |

**Table 1.4**    BDA for Independent Application of Schemata

---

**NCTE Standards:**

**1.**  Students read a wide range of print and nonprint texts to build an understanding of texts, of themselves, and of the cultures of the United States and the world; to acquire new information; to respond to the needs and demands of society and the workplace; and for personal fulfillment. Among these texts are fiction and nonfiction, classic and contemporary works.

**3.**  Students apply a wide range of strategies to comprehend, interpret, evaluate, and appreciate texts. They draw on their prior experience, their interactions with other readers and writers, their knowledge of word meaning and of other texts, their word identification strategies, and their understanding of textual features (e.g., sound-letter correspondence, sentence structure, context, graphics).

---

**Picture Book:** Students self-select their text. See resources for suggested titles.

| | | | |
|---|---|---|---|
| **Before** | High ↕ Low | **Teacher** *Remember when you read _____, _____, _____, and _____ and used your prior knowledge to guide your understanding? As you independently read _____ back at your seat, you may choose to use the T-Chart or sticky notes as you use your prior knowledge to make connections.* | Self-selects a piece of literature at each independent level. **Student** |
| **During** | High ↕ Low | In between small group instruction and/or during transition time, evaluate students' use of prior knowledge. Make sure prior knowledge is appropriate and connections enhance students' understanding. Make anecdotal notes when and for whom this process breaks down. Use the notes to adjust small group instruction. **Teacher** | Reads _____ and records prior knowledge and connections. **Student** |
| **After** | High ↕ Low | Ask for student volunteers to share their T-Charts and share how their prior knowledge developed their understanding. **Teacher** | **Student** Shares T-Chart. |

The teacher must consider:

- Readers' present strategies
- Readers' interests and background knowledge
- Text complexity in relation to readers' current skills
- Language of the text in relation to readers' experience
- Content of the text in relation to readers' background knowledge
- Appropriateness of the content to the age group
- Representation of gender, racial, ethnic, and socioeconomic groups in positive ways
- Teacher's assessment of the learning opportunities inherent in a text and their match to the established instructional goals
- Quality of the text: language, illustrations, layout, writing style (Fountas & Pinnell, 2001, p. 223, 2001)

## SUMMARY

- Prior knowledge encompasses the readers' experiences with text and life.
- Prior knowledge must be activated efficiently.
- Proficient readers constantly change their schemata based upon the newly required knowledge.

Before continuing on your thinking adventure, stop and reflect . . .

**Table 1.5**

| Make your thinking visible . . . | | |
|---|---|---|
| **Reflection Questions:** | *Why is it critical for me to demonstrate how my prior knowledge continues to grow? How do my students manage their changing schema?* | |
| **Modeling Through Think Aloud** — High ↕ Low | **Teacher** | **Student** |
| **Guided Practice** — High ↕ Low | **Teacher** | **Student** |
| **Independent Application** — High ↕ Low | **Teacher** | **Student** |

# 2 Interacting With the Text

## *Questioning*

*Tell me, I'll forget. Show me, I may remember. But involve me and I'll understand.*

—Chinese proverb

Watching students bring their thinking alive is an exciting process to behold. For some, they may formulate new ideas or concepts. Along with their newfound thoughts, teachers may also realize they need other resources to clarify meaning. For others, listening to student questions may lead to new horizons of thinking too (Langer, 1995). Questioning leads to the understanding of relationships between other comprehension strategies. By asking questions we begin to clearly see the picture the author has created; we weed out unimportant facts to help determine important ideas; we reorganize our schema so new ideas are reconnected; we readjust our understanding of text, text features, and text structures to help us monitor our reading behaviors. Questioning is the patriarch of the comprehension family, holding our thinking together. Observing how students interact with text and one another is the active process of comprehending (Farr, 2002). Reading is definitely thinking.

In Audrey's second grade inclusion classroom, the students are seated on the floor, watching as I aim and throw the ball at an unresponsive participant. Laughing, they begin to wonder why their teacher doesn't catch the ball. Continuing several more times, Audrey finally catches the ball and we begin throwing the ball back and forth, around our backs, and we even manage to lob a few. I ask the students which looked like more fun? They all chime in, "When you both were catching the ball." We sit down and I begin to share with Audrey's students how reading is like playing catch with the author. Authors provide us with thousands of words on the page. They remain only words unless we actively think about the relationship between the words. Words can tell a story, clarify facts about a certain topic, create images, recall moments in time, and account for documenting facts. We take the author's words and connect those events or topics to our own experiences. To return the ball back to the author, we have to ask ourselves questions to clarify or bring new meaning to those connections. Active thinking is an author-reader interaction—tossing ideas and questions back and forth in order to construct a very meaningful, personal message.

In a third grade inclusion classroom, Carol has a familiar big book on the floor and she is literally standing on the book *The Three Billy Goats Gruff.* She has a playground ball and she bounces the ball on the words. As the ball hits the page and bounces back, Carol shares with her students how the words from the book develop into an event, create characters by their actions or words, or build a picture in our heads by the simple words of "trip-trap, trip-trap." These words remain one-dimensional until we ask questions to gain further information about the story. By throwing the ball back to the author with our question(s) in mind, we begin to create those multidimensional levels of understanding (see Table 2.1 on the next page).

Inviting some of her other students to "play catch," Carol asks them to stand around the big book. Making a text-to-text connection, another student wonders why authors such as Lois Elhert use onomatopoeia in their writing. Another student adds to the connection and clarifies by saying, "Authors use those kinds of words to create a sound in our heads." Here Carol's students have a film in their heads of what thinking and reading look like and sound like. They can visually see the distribution of meaning between friends, teacher, and author.

With Kathy's fourth grade Title 1 students, we have already modeled Playing Catch With the Author with several books by Patricia Polacco noticing the relationships between personal experiences, elements of story, and author's craft. Watching and listening, the students see how many questions I have before and during reading. They begin to notice those lingering questions, which aren't answered but still trouble us for solutions (see Table 2.2 on page 36).

After school, Kathy and I begin to reflect upon the students' excitement over the amount of questions one can have on one page of text; they see it is alright to have questions that are not answered, and they have difficulty holding their questions inside. We knew we were ready to invite them into guided practice with our next book *The Summer My Father Was Ten,* by Pat Brisson.

**Table 2.1**

| NCTE Standards: |
|---|
| **1.** Students read a wide range of print and nonprint texts to build an understanding of texts, of themselves, and of the cultures of the United States and the world; to acquire new information; to respond to the needs and demands of society and the workplace; and for personal fulfillment. Among these texts are fiction and nonfiction, classic and contemporary works. |
| **3.** Students apply a wide range of strategies to comprehend, interpret, evaluate, and appreciate texts. They draw on their prior experience, their interactions with other readers and writers, their knowledge of word meaning and of other texts, their word identification strategies, and their understanding of textual features (e.g., sound-letter correspondence, sentence structure, context, graphics). |

**Guiding Question:** *How will questioning enable my students to interact with the author's words?*

| | | |
|---|---|---|
| **Modeling Through Think Aloud** — High ↕ Low | **Teacher**<br>Build an understanding of how questioning leads to comprehending and how it supports the reorganization of ideas and concepts. | Activates prior knowledge and listens to the types of questions being asked.<br><br>**Student** |
| **Guided Practice** — High ↕ Low | Continue to build an understanding of how questioning leads to comprehending and how it supports the reorganization of ideas and concepts.<br><br>**Teacher** | Continues to activate prior knowledge and begins to ask questions for clarification, confirmation or rejection of predictions, reorganization of schema, and for word meanings.<br><br>**Student** |
| **Independent Application** — High ↕ Low | Monitor students' abilities to ask questions and continue to monitor their prior knowledge and understanding of text.<br>**Teacher** | **Student**<br>Continues to build upon prior knowledge and asks questions to comprehend. |

The next day, I read, as Kathy writes the students' questions down in a journal. I continue reading and responding to a few. Again students begin to notice some of their questions are answered right away and some are answered further into the story. At the end of the day, Kathy charts their questions and shares how she will manage this part of the lesson without

**Figure 2.1**

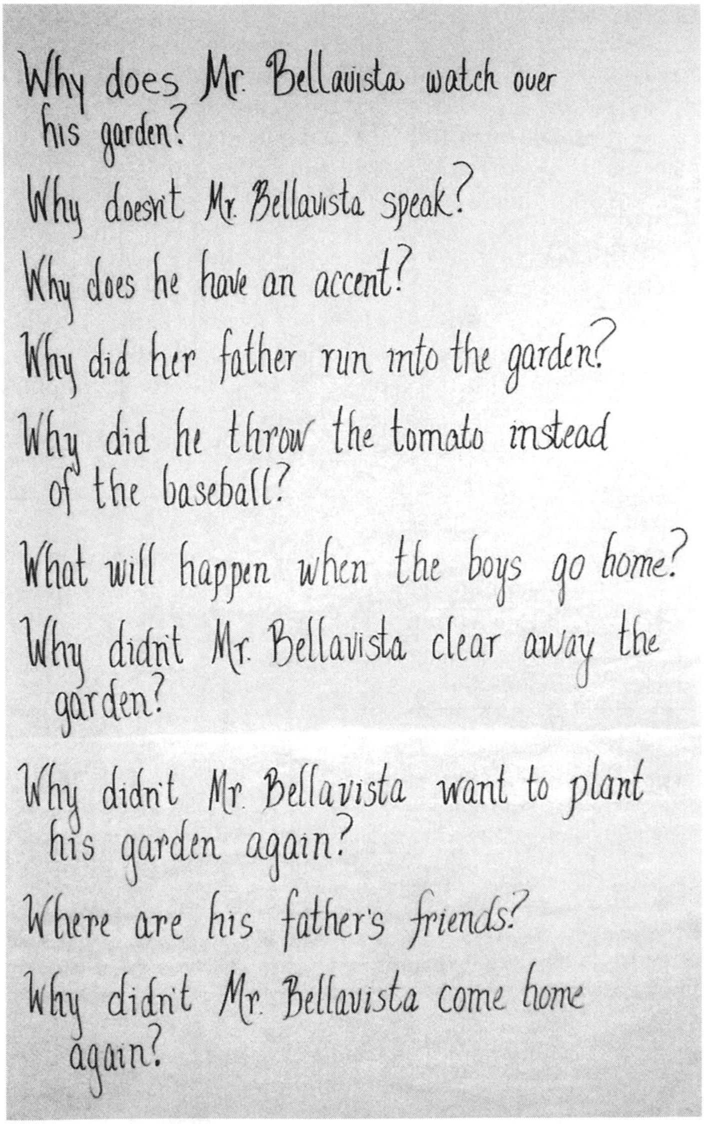

Why does Mr. Bellavista watch over his garden?

Why doesn't Mr. Bellavista speak?

Why does he have an accent?

Why did her father run into the garden?

Why did he throw the tomato instead of the baseball?

What will happen when the boys go home?

Why didn't Mr. Bellavista clear away the garden?

Why didn't Mr. Bellavista want to plant his garden again?

Where are his father's friends?

Why didn't Mr. Bellavista come home again?

my assistance. While listening to the story, Kathy says she will pause periodically throughout the Read Aloud and allow time for her students to write their questions on Post-it notes. After hearing the story, Kathy will set up a chart, or an area on the board, for students to display their questions. In fact, she thinks this will provide a wonderful opportunity for students to view other students' thinking.

The next day, we revisit their questions by coding the questions that were answered within the text and questions that were answered by the author's words and the students' inferences. We continue this process for several days.

**Figure 2.2**

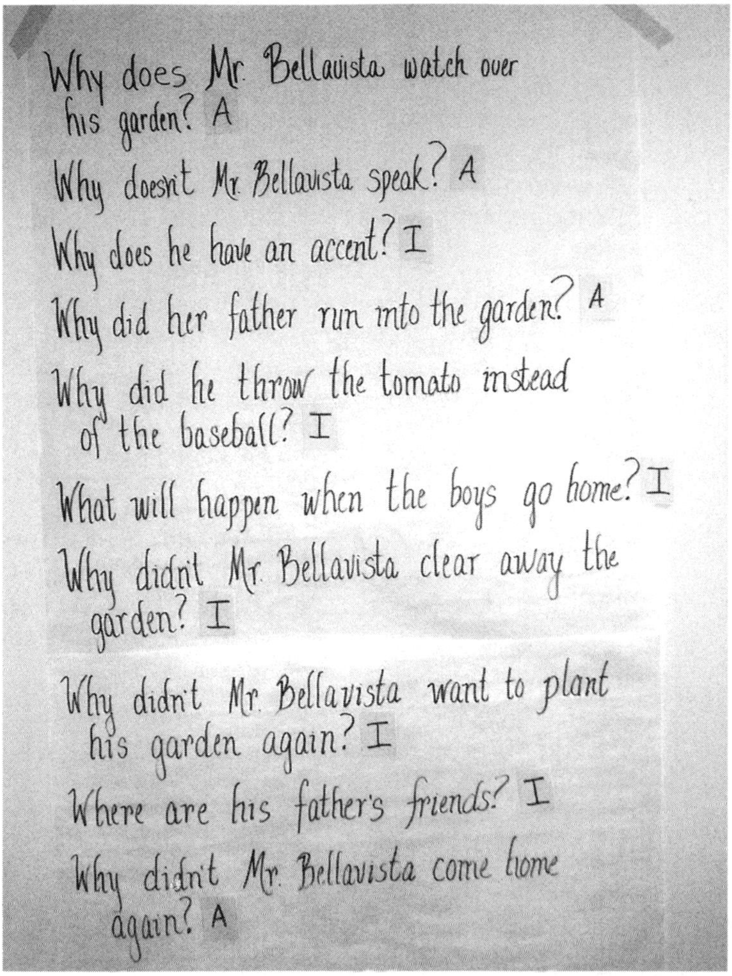

Why does Mr. Bellavista watch over his garden? A

Why doesn't Mr. Bellavista speak? A

Why does he have an accent? I

Why did her father run into the garden? A

Why did he throw the tomato instead of the baseball? I

What will happen when the boys go home? I

Why didn't Mr. Bellavista clear away the garden? I

Why didn't Mr. Bellavista want to plant his garden again? I

Where are his father's friends? I

Why didn't Mr. Bellavista come home again? A

Continuing working with Kathy and her students, we select several texts by Patricia Polacco to read: *Thank You, Mr. Falker, Chicken Sunday, My Red-Headed Brother,* and *Thundercakes.* Using these texts, we continue the process of charting questions and noticing which questions can be answered immediately and which questions need our prior knowledge.

## GUIDING STUDENTS' THINKING

Meanwhile, in Jonathan's third grade suburban classroom, his students have carefully observed his effective, explicit questioning instruction. They are ready to be released into the next phase of learning—guided practice. He gives each student Post-it notes to record their questions as they read *Miss Rumphius* by Barbara Cooney.

(Text Continues on Page 41)

**Table 2.2** BDA for Teacher Modeling Questioning

---

**NCTE Standards:**

1. Students read a wide range of print and nonprint texts to build an understanding of texts, of themselves, and of the cultures of the United States and the world; to acquire new information; to respond to the needs and demands of society and the workplace; and for personal fulfillment. Among these texts are fiction and nonfiction, classic and contemporary works.

3. Students apply a wide range of strategies to comprehend, interpret, evaluate, and appreciate texts. They draw on their prior experience, their interactions with other readers and writers, their knowledge of word meaning and of other texts, their word identification strategies, and their understanding of textual features (e.g., sound-letter correspondence, sentence structure, context, graphics).

---

**Picture Book:** *The Summer My Father Was Ten* by Pat Brisson

| | | **Teacher** | |
|---|---|---|---|
| **Before** | High ↕ Low | Read title<br><br>*I think the title is telling us how this story will be about one moment in time.*<br><br>*Looking at the front cover, I wonder if the story is going to be about baseball or about some other event?*<br><br>*The illustrator gives us very little clues to the story line.*<br><br>*We do know that the story has a significant time and place.*<br><br>*As I read <u>The Summer My Father was Ten</u>, I want to share my questions with you.* | Activates prior knowledge, thinks about the questions being asked and begins to formulate some ideas about the story.<br><br><br><br><br><br><br><br>**Student** |
| **During** | High ↕ Low | Begin reading text aloud.<br>Pause at the end of the 2nd page.<br>*I wonder why her father tells her the same story.*<br>Continue reading to the bottom of the 5th page.<br>**Teacher** | **Student**<br>Activate prior knowledge, thinks about the questions being asked and begins to formulate some ideas about the story. |

*We know now Mr. Bellavista enjoys planting a garden, he enjoys listening to the radio, he has an accent, and he doesn't talk much to other folks.*

*I wonder why Mr. Bellavista is such a stranger to his neighbors?*

Continue to the end of the 9th page.

*Wow, now we see how one event can lead to another and cause harm for all. The boys certainly got carried away with their behaviors. Will Mr. Bellavista catch them in the act?*

*What kind of trouble will the boys get into? Will Mr. Bellavista call their parents?*

Continue reading to the bottom of the 13th page.

*After the other boys left the field, the girl's father could see how the garden was trampled and ruined. He could also see the hurt and hear the disgust in Mr. Bellavista's voice. Why wouldn't her father go over and apologize, or try to explain what happened? Why do you think, "his feet were like heavy stone?" What do you think Mr. Bellavista is thinking? Do you think Mr. Bellavista will replant his garden?*

*(Continued)*

**Table 2.2** (Continued)

| | | |
|---|---|---|
| | Continue reading to the bottom of the 18th page. *We know her father is feeling very guilty, but what are his friends thinking and where are they? Why is her father the one so worried?* Continue reading to the end of the 22nd page. *I wonder if her father is still feeling guilty. I wonder if Mr. Bellavista will trust her father again.* Finish reading the story. *Her father continues to plant a garden for six more years and carries on the tradition. I wonder if she will carry on the tradition of planting a garden and telling a story when she becomes a parent.* | |
| **After** High ↕ Low | *As you listened to the story and my questions, you can see how I was playing "catch with the author." Tomorrow, we will revisit my questions so we can see how many questions can be answered. Do you think questions can help us develop a better understanding of the story? I still have all these questions swimming around in my head. And look, we have finished reading but I am still playing "catch with the author."* **Teacher** | **Student** Actively listens |

## Student One

**Figure 2.3**

Why did Alice have to make the
world more beautiful?

Why do they call her Miss Rump-
kius now?

How did she did it?

## Student Two

**Figure 2.4**

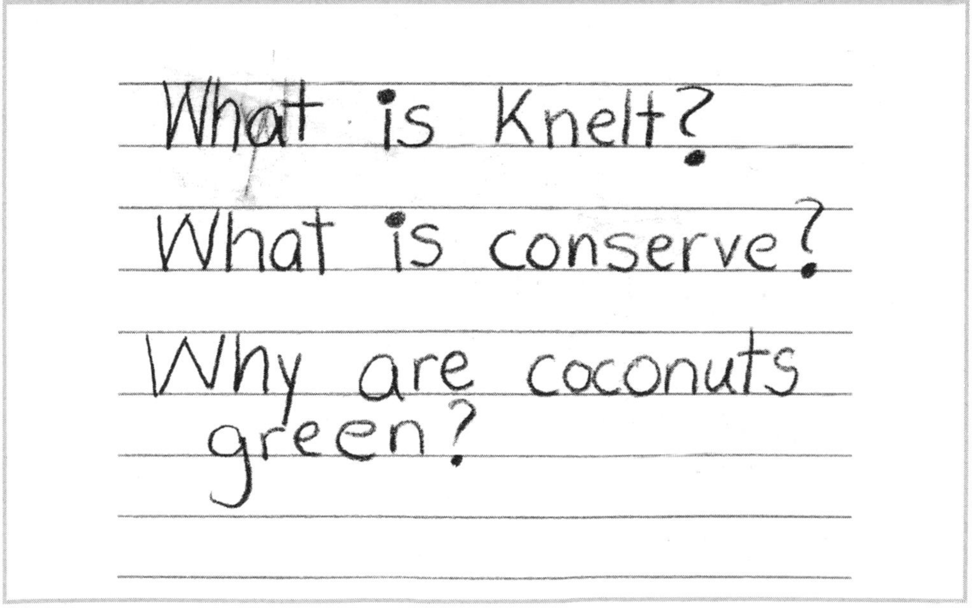

What is Knelt?

What is conserve?

Why are coconuts
green?

**Student Three**

Figure 2.5

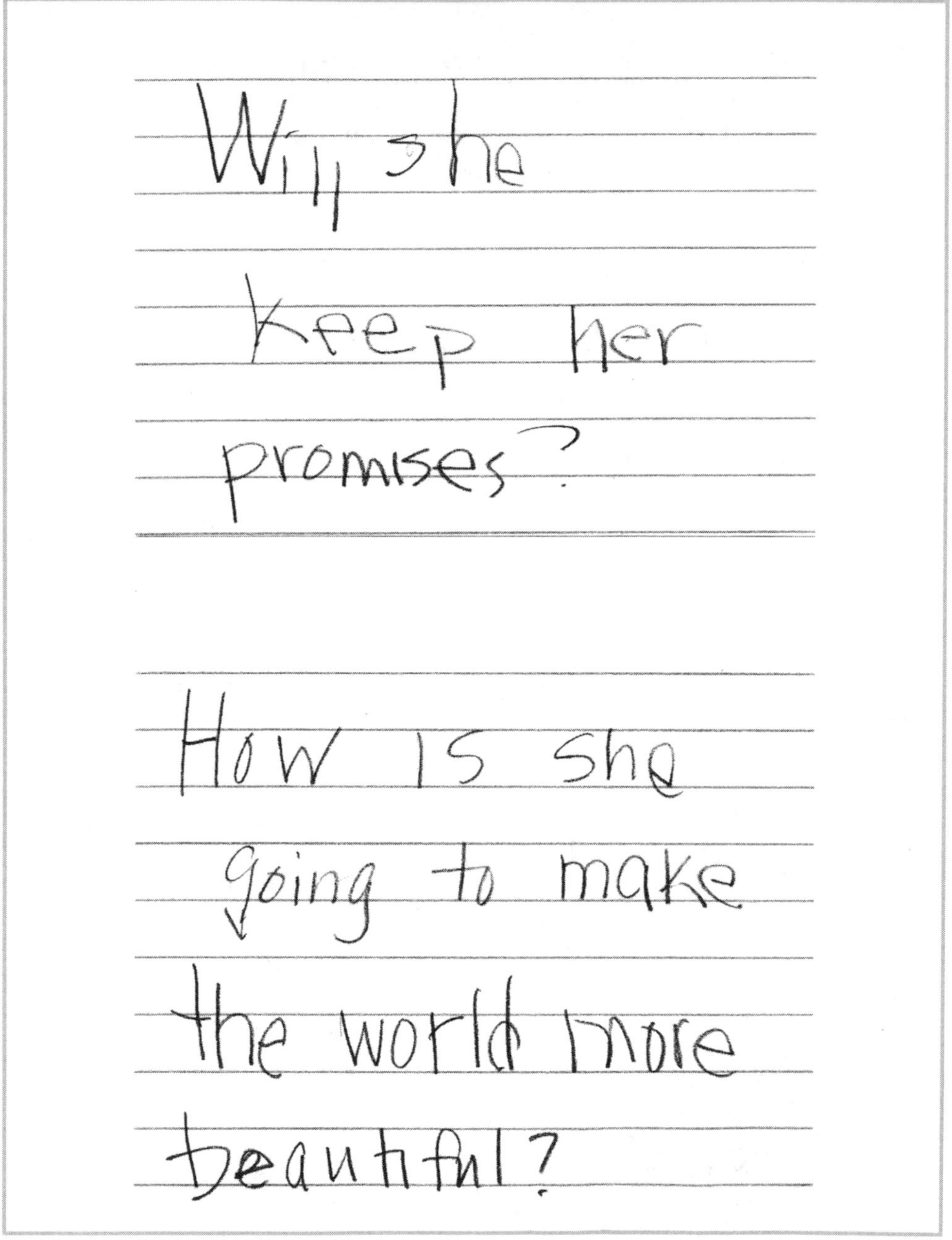

Will she

keep her

promises?

How is she

going to make

the world more

beautiful?

By reviewing these questions, Jonathan determines what type of instruction his students need next. For example, Student One and Student Three are ready to be released into the independent application phase. Student Two needs further guided practice. Jonathan decides to provide some more modeling, using *Two Bad Ants* by Chris Van Allsburg. As Jonathan provides more exemplary examples, he focuses on using "I wonder" as a sentence starter. Student Two's level of questioning improves enough to help him increase his understanding.

## Student Two

**Figure 2.6**

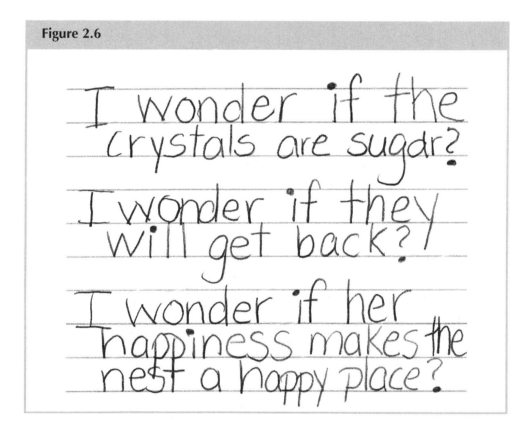

Finally, after seven days of guided practice, Jonathan releases all of his students into the independent application phase. Students One, Two, and Three read Cynthia Rylant's *The Bird House*.

**Student One**

Figure 2.7

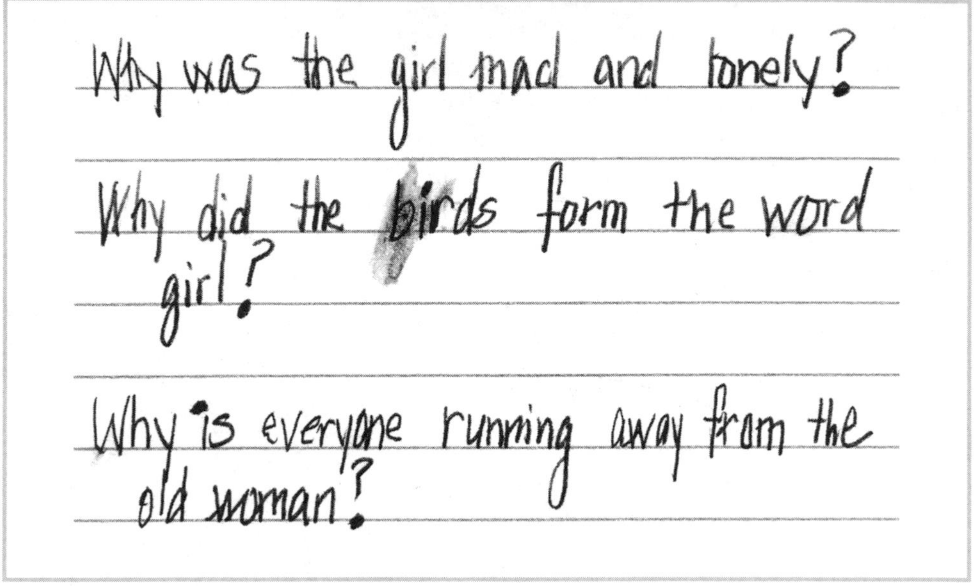

Why was the girl mad and lonely?

Why did the birds form the word girl?

Why is everyone running away from the old woman?

**Student Two**

Figure 2.8

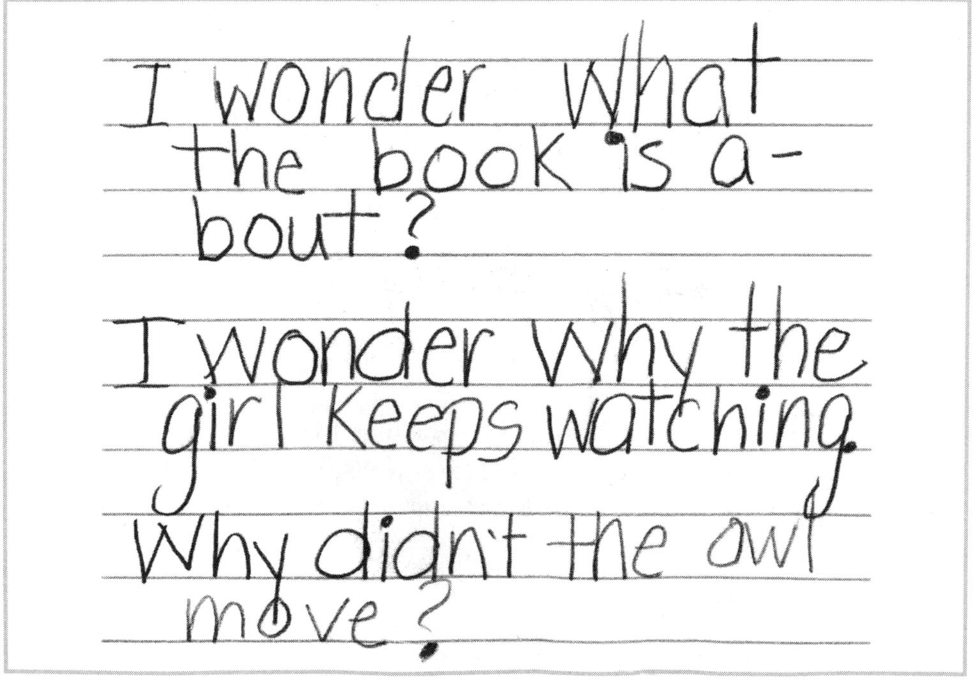

I wonder what the book is a-bout?

I wonder why the girl keeps watching.

Why didn't the owl move?

**Student Three**

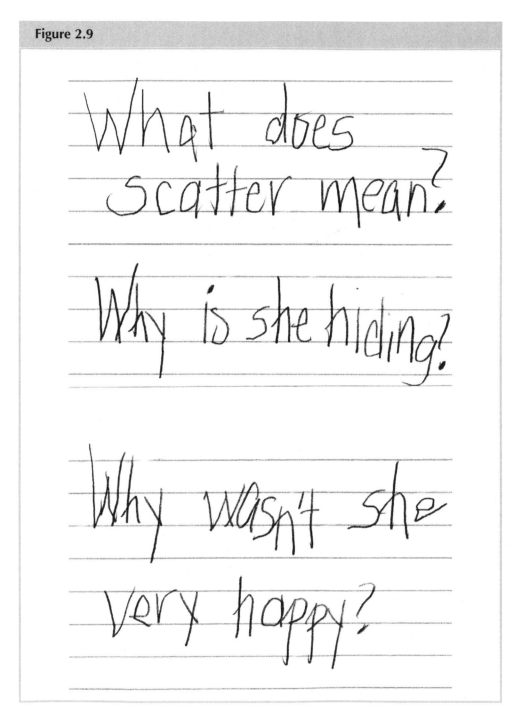

Figure 2.9

What does scatter mean?

Why is she hiding?

Why wasn't she very happy?

The next framework will assist you as you plan the guided practice phase of your instruction.

**Table 2.3**

| NCTE Standards: |
| --- |
| **1.** Students read a wide range of print and nonprint texts to build an understanding of texts, of themselves, and of the cultures of the United States and the world; to acquire new information; to respond to the needs and demands of society and the workplace; and for personal fulfillment. Among these texts are fiction and nonfiction, classic and contemporary works.<br><br>**3.** Students apply a wide range of strategies to comprehend, interpret, evaluate, and appreciate texts. They draw on their prior experience, their interactions with other readers and writers, their knowledge of word meaning and of other texts, their word identification strategies, and their understanding of textual features (e.g., sound-letter correspondence, sentence structure, context, graphics). |

| **Picture Book:** *The Summer My Father Was Ten* by Pat Brisson | | |
| --- | --- | --- |
| **Before**<br><br>High<br>↑<br>↓<br>Low | **Teacher**<br>*After you left yesterday, I charted all the questions that I had while reading* The Summer My Father was Ten. *As I reread the story today, see if you can "play catch with the author." If you have some questions too, we can add your questions in a different color. Do you think you might have some questions? Revisit each of these questions and see if we can answer them together.* | Activates prior knowledge, thinks about the questions being asked and begins to formulate his or her own questions.<br><br><br><br><br><br><br><br><br><br>**Student** |
| **During**<br><br>High<br>↑<br>↓<br>Low | Read the text, pausing to answer questions and to add students' thinking/questions.<br><br>Listen for misinformation and note those students who have difficulty participating.<br><br>Code the questions that can't be answered, and think about the types of questions the students predominantly ask.<br><br>**Teacher** | Student examples:<br><br>*Why does Mr. Bellavista watch over his garden?*<br>*Why doesn't Mr. Bellavista speak?*<br><br>*Why does he have an accent?*<br><br>*Why did her father run into the garden?*<br><br>*Why did the boys throw the tomato instead of the baseball?*<br><br>*What will happen when the boys go home?* |

| | | | |
|---|---|---|---|
| | | | *Why did Mr. Bellavista clear away the garden?*<br><br>*Why didn't Mr. Bellavista want to plant his garden again?*<br><br>*Where are her father's friends?*<br><br>*Why didn't Mr. Bellavista come home again?*<br><br>**Student** |
| **After** | High<br><br>↑<br>↓<br><br>Low | Revisit the chart, highlighting the number of questions and also the questions which led to a deeper understanding of the text. (This will vary according to student responses.)<br><br>**Teacher** | **Student**<br>Actively answers and questions the author's words and responses from other students and teacher. |

# GRADUALLY RELEASING STUDENTS INTO SELF-QUESTIONING

Gradually releasing the responsibility to the students, we ask them to apply questioning to their independent reading. Selecting independent text, we want to see if they can make connections and apply questioning to their readings. We give them Post-it notes to use and have them mark the Post-it note with a question mark to signal their thinking. We monitor their behaviors very closely by providing support during this time. Having the students begin reading for five minutes, we notice which students mark their pages with Post-it notes. Conferencing with those students, we acknowledge their questions but realize we need to model again in our Think Aloud, and perhaps quantify the questions that can't be answered immediately. Most of their questions are one-dimensional or stand-alone questions. One-dimensional questions are those literal questions that can be answered immediately and simply. Collectively these questions may lead to a deeper meaning. For example, by gathering all of the literal questions about a particular character, providing and

**Table 2.4**

| NCTE Standards: |
|---|
| **1.** Students read a wide range of print and nonprint texts to build an understanding of texts, of themselves, and of the cultures of the United States and the world; to acquire new information; to respond to the needs and demands of society and the workplace; and for personal fulfillment. Among these texts are fiction and nonfiction, classic and contemporary works.<br><br>**3.** Students apply a wide range of strategies to comprehend, interpret, evaluate, and appreciate texts. They draw on their prior experience, their interactions with other readers and writers, their knowledge of word meaning and of other texts, their word identification strategies, and their understanding of textual features (e.g., sound-letter correspondence, sentence structure, context, graphics). |

| **Picture Book:** Students self-select their text. See Resources for suggested titles. | | |
|---|---|---|
| **Before**<br>High<br>↕<br>Low | **Teacher**<br>*Remember when we read together _____, _____, _____, and _____ and we asked questions for building a deeper meaning? As you independently read _____ back at your seat, you may want to write your questions on sticky notes. This way, I can see where and what you are thinking.* | Self-selects a piece of literature at independent level.<br><br><br><br><br><br><br><br><br>**Student** |
| **During**<br>High<br>↕<br>Low | In between small group instruction and/or during transition time, evaluate the students' use of prior knowledge and questioning. Make sure prior knowledge is appropriate and connections enhance their understanding. Notice the types of questions being asked. You may want to make anecdotal notes when and for whom this process breaks down. You will use the notes to adjust small group instruction.<br><br>**Teacher** | Reads _____ and records prior knowledge and connections.<br><br><br><br><br><br><br><br><br><br><br><br><br><br>**Student** |

| | | Student |
|---|---|---|
| High ↕ Low | During transition time, ask for volunteers to share their sketches and their thinking. | Orally shares thinking and sketches. (Sketches may be shared on a Graffiti Door/Wall, or a large blank sheet of white paper taped to a door or wall. Students write the title of their story and attach the sketch they created during independent reading.) |
| | Teacher | |

linking the answers together, we then can explicitly model how to take this new information and draw a conclusion about the character's behaviors and interactions. As with any strategy instruction, it is a continuous process of revisiting and combining strategy within strategy.

## SUMMARY

- Questioning is the centrifugal force of comprehension.
- Questioning promotes intimate conversations between reader and text.
- Questioning clarifies the reader's ideas and deepens his/her understanding.
- Questioning sets up a dialogue with the author.

Before continuing on your thinking adventure, stop and reflect . . .

**Table 2.5**

| Make your thinking visible . . . | | |
|---|---|---|
| **Reflection Questions:** | *How did my questioning lead to deeper meaning? How does deeper meaning help students interact with the author?* | |
| **Modeling Through Think Aloud** High ↕ Low | **Teacher** | **Student** |
| **Guided Practice** High ↕ Low | **Teacher** | **Student** |
| **Independent Application** High ↕ Low | **Teacher** | **Student** |

# 3

# Directing a Movie in Your Mind

*Visualizing*

*If books could be more, could show more, could own more, this book would smell . . .*

—Gary Paulsen's *The Winter Room*

Entering Pam's first grade inclusion classroom, students are quite busy creating and sharing their creative images from the read aloud, *Fireflies.* Jarrod lounges in his chair and closes his eyes—his face lights up as he envisions using a mason jar to capture the fireflies in the summer night. Jonathan's pencil races across his paper as he sketches the fireflies circling in the night sky. Gibson smiles as he uses his Model Magic to create a flying firefly on his black mat. A good book draws children in, makes them think, sparks curiosity, and opens the doors to their imagination. These young readers are able to use the descriptive language Julie Brinkloe expertly shares in *Fireflies* to have their personal interaction with her words. Visualization helps us notice details and to create the sensory images that the writer is trying to portray. The mental picture we develop while we read is a kind of inferential thinking that connects with the questions we have generated and the prior knowledge we have acquired (Cooper & Kiger, 2006).

Reflect on your own experiences, especially when you read a Pulitzer Prize winner such as Sonia Nazario's *Enrique's Journey.*

*The train passes into northern Chiapas. Enrique sees men with hoes tending their corn and women inside their kitchens patting tortillas into shape. Cowboys ride past and smile. Fieldworkers wave their machetes and cheer the migrants on: "Qué bueno!" Mountains draw closer. Plantain fields soften into cow pastures. Enriques's train slows to a crawl. Monarch butterflies flutter alongside, overtaking his car.*

*As the sun sets and the oppressive heat breaks, he hears crickets and frogs begin their music and join the migrant chorus. The moon rises. Thousands of fireflies flicker around the train. Stars come out to shine, so many they seem jammed together, brilliant points of light all across the sky. (2006, p. 87)*

- Were you able to make a picture in your mind of this scene? Describe what you see, hear, feel, smell and taste.
- Using your prior knowledge, did you add some details that are not in Nazario's book?
- How did this mental image enhance your construction of meaning?

## MENTAL IMAGERY

Research suggests that mental imagery is a strategy that can play an important and positive role in enhancing reading comprehension (Block & Pressley, 2002). When readers make mental images about information and stories, these mental "pictures" provide the framework for organizing and remembering the text. We are successful with mental imagery only if we link prior knowledge with textual information.

What prior knowledge did you activate to construct your mental image? Many students do not spontaneously use mental imagery as a comprehension strategy, but will do so if supported by the teacher (Block & Pressley, 2002). In order to create an awareness of the value of imagery, Block and Pressley (2002) have four recommendations to consider when instructing. First, teachers need to use high-image-evoking text to allow students opportunities to create images. Second, teachers need to offer opportunities to recall these images during group discussions. Third, teachers need to inform students that mental imagery will assist them in understanding difficult text by modeling this strategy through Think Alouds. Last, teachers need to inform students that mental imagery can facilitate their writing.

In order to develop readers who demonstrate visualization competently, we must scaffold their acquisition of this complex cognitive strategy. Fredericks (1986) and Barclay (1990) recommend using a sequence of six activities to develop the awareness of using imagery as a cognitive strategy:

1. Provide students with opportunities to create images of concrete objects.
   - In Pam's first grade classroom, she asks her students to put their crayon box on their desktops. She has them study the boxes by checking out all sides of the boxes, smelling the boxes, lifting the boxes, studying the undersides, and so on. She then asks the students to find their study buddy. Buddy I must close his or her eyes and describe the mental image to the study buddy. Then Buddy II has an opportunity to share his or her mental image.

2. Provide opportunities for guided imagery of concrete objects.
   - At this point in the sequence, Pam asks the class to close their eyes and create a mental image of a dog. Pam tells the students that the dog is white with black spots. He has floppy ears. His fur is very soft. He sits in their laps with his head resting on their knees. Students give her thumbs up when they have painted the dog in their minds.

3. Encourage students to recall familiar objects or scenes.
   - Pam continues to develop the awareness of her students' knowledge of visualization as she asks students to create a mental picture of the outside of the school. After students have their images designed in their minds, she gives them paper and colored pencils to sketch the school. Once students complete their drawings, they take a walking field trip outside and compare their pictures to the part of the building they drew.

4. Provide guided instruction to support students in making images of events and actions.
   - Pam is very impressed with her students' ability to talk about their images. Even though they are not the world's greatest artists, the students are able to share their mental images in the discussions. Pam therefore decides it is time to move on in the sequence. She asks students to think back to the dog they imagined earlier. "He is still lying on your lap," she assures them. "But now the front door opens and a gust of cold air rushes in. Your dog jumps off your lap and lands on the floor. He scampers off behind the sofa, and lies next to the heat vent." Her students' giggle as they continue to paint this "movie" in their minds.

5. Develop the use of imagery in listening situations.
   - Pam realizes that her students need to sustain their visualizations as they listen to a very descriptive text. She selects Julie Brinkloe's *Fireflies*. As she begins, she reminds them that it is time for her to make her dream come true and become a movie producer. At this point in the sequence Pam decides her students have a strong awareness of the cognitive strategy visualization. She proceeds to

**Table 3.1**

| | | |
|---|---|---|
| **NCTE Standards:** | | |

**NCTE Standards:**

**1.** Students read a wide range of print and nonprint texts to build an understanding of texts, of themselves, and of the cultures of the United States and the world; to acquire new information; to respond to the needs and demands of society and the workplace; and for personal fulfillment. Among these texts are fiction and nonfiction, classic and contemporary works.

**3.** Students apply a wide range of strategies to comprehend, interpret, evaluate, and appreciate texts. They draw on their prior experience, their interactions with other readers and writers, their knowledge of word meaning and of other texts, their word identification strategies, and their understanding of textual features (e.g., sound-letter correspondence, sentence structure, context, graphics).

**Guiding Question**: *How will students be able to use their prior knowledge and imaging skills to create dynamic visualizations?*

| | | |
|---|---|---|
| **Modeling Through Think Aloud** — High ↕ Low | **Teacher** Build an understanding of the author's descriptive language, the reader's background experiences, and the importance of dynamic mental images. | Develops an awareness of the importance of dynamic mental images. **Student** |
| **Guided Practice** — High ↕ Low | Continue to build an understanding of the author's descriptive language, the reader's background experiences, and the importance of dynamic mental images. **Teacher** | Begins to activate prior knowledge and changes mental images as the story progresses. **Student** |
| **Independent Application** — High ↕ Low | Monitor students' understanding of the author's descriptive language, students' background experiences, and understanding the importance of dynamic mental images. **Teacher** | **Student** Activates prior knowledge and realizes the importance of changing mental images as the story progresses. |

model her visualization as she reads *Fireflies*. Pam uses Table 3.1 to plan her series of visualization lessons.

6. Provide instructions to encourage students to use the illustrations provided within a text to help them create their own images of the events and actions in the story.

## Modeling for Intermediate Readers

In Gretchen's fourth grade rural classroom, she decides to use *Harvey Potter's Balloon Farm* by Jerdine Nolen to demonstrate the idea of creating a mental image, comparing it with the illustrator's interpretation of the text,

**Figure 3.1**

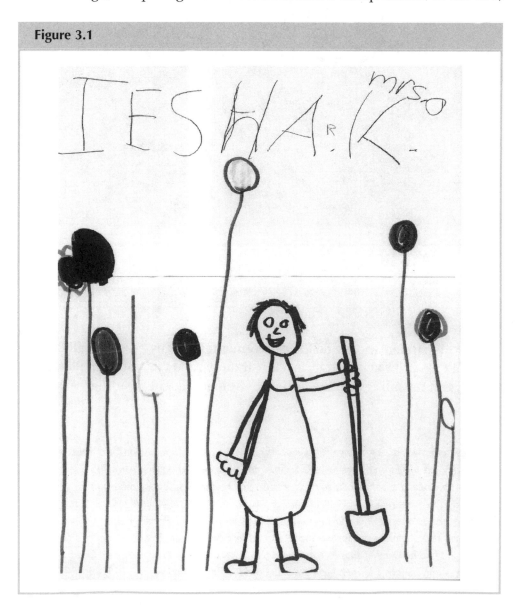

**Figure 3.2**

then asking students to refine their own mental images based on all of this information—prior knowledge, text illustrations, and current mental images.

Without revealing the illustrations, Gretchen begins reading.

*Harvey Potter was a very strange fellow indeed. He was a farmer, but he didn't like farming like my daddy did. He farmed a genuine, U.S. Government Inspected Balloon Farm. No one knew exactly how he did it. Some folks say that it wasn't real—that it was magic. But I know what I say, and those were real, actual balloons growing out of the plain ole ground! Harvey Potter had some of the prettiest colors you'd ever want to see on a balloon. Pleasin' Purple, Orange-Ray Sun, Yellin' Yellow. There was Rip-Two-Shot Red, and Jelly-Bean Black, Bloomin' Blue, and Grassy Green. He had all kinds of shapes, too. Round balloons. Long ones. Animal shapes. Clowns with big noses and mouths. He even grew great big sharp teeth for Halloween. (1998, pp. 2–4)*

Then Gretchen says, "Now snap that picture in your minds! I want you to sketch your balloon farm on your paper." Students share their drawings with one another. They quickly notice how they differ from one another.

Gretchen proceeds to explain that since each child has different experiences with balloons and farms, their mental images vary. She also shares Mark Buehner's interpretation of the text—his illustrations are even more different! Gretchen explains, "There is no right or wrong way to visualize; it is your turn to produce your personal movie of the story you are reading." She reminds her class:

> When good readers read they ask themselves questions. Does the author use any describing words that help me paint a picture in my mind? Does what I read remind me of anything in my life? What do I see, hear, smell, feel, and taste? If we ask ourselves these questions as we read, we can create many dynamic mental images in our minds, which will help us remember and understand what we are reading.

(See Table 3.2 to see how Gretchen models visualization for her students.) Just as Gretchen models this lesson with her fourth graders, Crystal spends several days modeling her personal movie production of *The Salamander Room* for her at-risk first graders. Crystal determines they are ready to move into the guided practice phase of visualization, based upon the feedback from her class. However, Crystal wants to be sure that her students are aware that visualization is a dynamic cognitive strategy; their mental images need to change throughout the story. Crystal chooses to use *The Napping House* (Wood, 1984) next because it will allow the students multiple opportunities to change their mental pictures as they gain more information. As the story develops, more sleeping characters are added to the cozy bed. At the end of the story, the wakeful flea is placed on top of the cozy bed and then chaos erupts in the sleeping house. The story allows for rich discussions about what will happen next in the story and how our images are different from one another. In addition, Crystal feels this text is developmentally appropriate for first graders, as they understand the language and the concepts. The verse is expanding; however, each page repeats the list of people and animals sleeping on the bed, effectively cementing those images in their mental pictures. See Table 3.3 to learn how Crystal scaffolds her students' learning as she provides guided practice with visualization.

*(Text Continues on Page 60)*

**Table 3.2**

---

**NCTE Standards:**

**1.** Students read a wide range of print and nonprint texts to build an understanding of texts, of themselves, and of the cultures of the United States and the world; to acquire new information; to respond to the needs and demands of society and the workplace; and for personal fulfillment. Among these texts are fiction and nonfiction, classic and contemporary works.

**3.** Students apply a wide range of strategies to comprehend, interpret, evaluate, and appreciate texts. They draw on their prior experience, their interactions with other readers and writers, their knowledge of word meaning and of other texts, their word identification strategies, and their understanding of textual features (e.g., sound-letter correspondence, sentence structure, context, graphics).

---

**Picture Book:** *Owl Moon* by Jane Yolen

| | | **Teacher** | |
|---|---|---|---|
| **Before** | High ↕ Low | Read title and give a brief summary about the story. *Owl Moon is a story about a little girl and her father who go out in the middle of the night on an owling adventure.* *As I read Owl Moon, I want to share the mental images I create as I read.* | Activates prior knowledge, thinks about the illustration and begins to create mental images. |
| | | | **Student** |
| **During** | High ↕ Low | **Teacher** Begin reading text aloud. Pause after reading, "Our feet crunched over the crisp snow and little gray footsteps followed us. Pa made a long shadow, but mine was short and round. I had to run after him every now and then to keep up, and my short round, shadow bumped after me." Quickly sketch the image on the board while you explain the next phase. *As I read, I am picturing in my mind a very cold night. I know it must be cold because the author talks about snow. I see in my mind the little girl* | Students will activate their prior knowledge, think about the author's words, and begin to create mental images. Students will be able to compare their mental images with the teacher's sketches. |
| | | | **Student** |

*trailing after her tall father in very deep snow. I can hear the snow crunching with each step they take. I can feel the hard and frozen layer of ice covering the snow. This must be what the author means by "crisp snow." I also see the dark footprints that follow the little girl and her father, as I read the author's words "the little gray footsteps that followed us." In my head I can see the little girl turn around to see the footsteps that they've made in the snow. I also see shadows of different lengths. I already learned in science class that the shorter a person is, the shorter the shadow will be. I can hear the little girl huffing and puffing as she struggles to keep up with her father. It reminds me of how tired I got when I would chase after my older brother. I can even taste the cold snow that my brother would kick up in my face, the closer I got to him.*

Continue reading and pause after, "Then we came to a clearing in the woods. The moon was high above us. It seemed to fit exactly over the center of the clearing and the snow below; it was whiter than the milk in a bowl of cereal."
Quickly sketch another picture on the board while you explain the next phase.

*Jane Yolen uses the words, "Then we came to a clearing in the woods." In my head I see a wide open field somewhere in the middle of a forest. I can*

*(Continued)*

**Table 3.2** (Continued)

|  | *smell the pine trees surrounding the clearing. Ms. Yolen also describes the snow as being "whiter than the milk in a bowl of cereal." I imagine that everything is very white because the snow recently fell and nobody has walked in it yet. I know snow is very white because I grew up in Pennsylvania, where lots of white snow fell! I also remember that the snow would be really white only after it just fell and people or animals hadn't walked in it yet to make it dirty. In my mind, I feel a very cold wintry night. My movie shows a bright light in the center of the clearing. I think it's giving off a light because the moonlight is reflecting off the snow in the clearing. I'm thinking this because I sometimes go out in the snow at night, and the snow acts like a giant mirror to reflect the moon's beams.*<br><br>Continue reading and pause after, "I listened so hard my ears hurt and eyes got cloudy with the cold. Pa raised his face to call out again, but before he could open his mouth, an echo came threading its way through the trees." Quickly sketch another picture on the board while you explain the next phase.<br><br>*When Ms. Yolen uses the words, "I listened so hard my ears hurt" I can picture a little girl in the forest being very* |  |

*quiet while leaning her ear forward and straining to hear the sound of an owl. I can feel the tenseness that the little girl must be experiencing, as she listens so intently. I can feel the pain in my own ears. It reminds me of when I sometimes focus so hard on trying to hear someone speak who is very soft-spoken. I sometimes feel the pain in my own ears as I'm straining so hard to hear them speak. Ms. Yolen uses the words, "my eyes got cloudy with the cold." When I read those words, I could see in my head the same blurriness that the little girl must be experiencing as she looked into the trees. I know from personal experience that my eyes often get watery, and that it sometimes blurs my vision when it's very cold outside. In my movie I see the girl standing in the forest and suddenly hearing the sound of the giant horned owl flying from the trees to the sky above. I can hear his giant wings as they flap against the tree branches. The author says, "an echo came threading its way through the trees." I know that the girl and her father have finally heard the owl because they heard its echo. I know that it's easy to make an echo when you are in an enclosed area like a forest and it's very quiet all around you. I imagine hearing the echo of the sound made by the owl and I see it moving in and out of the trees as it tries to make its way to the sky above.*

Finish reading the story.

*(Continued)*

**Table 3.2** (Continued)

| | | Student |
|---|---|---|
| After High ↑ ↓ Low | *As I read the story, I used the author's descriptive words, my prior knowledge, and my senses to create my own movie. This is visualization. It's important to know that the images we make help us understand what is happening in the story.* <br> **Teacher** | Actively listens |

# TEACHER REFLECTIONS

After Crystal reviews the student work samples, she reflects on her instruction:

While I know that modeling is important, I can't say that I always did a great job at it! I think that incorporating the language of I Do, We Do, and You Do has been helpful in my lessons. First, it helps the students focus on their jobs during each component (a listener, a helper, and a doer, respectively). Also, I am trying to remain consistent in following those rules too. I am less likely now to jump right into You Do before they are ready for the independent practice. I think this was a successful lesson. The students were motivated, excited, and actively involved in the learning process. Even as I discussed the title, some of my students were bursting at the seams, wanting to share what they thought about and could see in their minds' eyes. As I continued reading the story, I could tell that some of them were playing their mental movies because they sat with their eyes closed on the carpet. For others, I could tell they were actively engaged because their hands were waving wildly in the air. For yet others, it was apparent in their giggles, laughs, and comments like "I can see it!" What impresses me most about my students' learning is the amount of details they include in the oral retelling of their mental images. For my reluctant writers and readers, this has provided a stress-free opportunity for them to share their knowledge with others and me. I think that as their confidence grows in their verbal abilities, it will carry over into their writing and reading. My struggling students are much better thinkers after this series of visualizing lessons. They are more cognizant of what they are reading, what it means, and how to make the words come alive in their minds. This has enabled them to think about what they might read next, instead of focusing just on decoding words. In addition, the

*(Text Continues on Page 65)*

**Table 3.3**

| NCTE Standards: |
| --- |
| **1.** Students read a wide range of print and nonprint texts to build an understanding of texts, of themselves, and of the cultures of the United States and the world; to acquire new information; to respond to the needs and demands of society and the workplace; and for personal fulfillment. Among these texts are fiction and nonfiction, classic and contemporary works.<br><br>**3.** Students apply a wide range of strategies to comprehend, interpret, evaluate, and appreciate texts. They draw on their prior experience, their interactions with other readers and writers, their knowledge of word meaning and of other texts, their word identification strategies, and their understanding of textual features (e.g., sound-letter correspondence, sentence structure, context, graphics). |

| **Picture Book:** *The Napping House* by Audrey Wood | | |
| --- | --- | --- |
| Before<br><br>High<br>↑<br>↓<br>Low | **Teacher**<br>*Today we are going to read The Napping House to continue learning about visualizing. Yesterday, I modeled for you. Today is a We Do day! I am going to give each of you a clipboard and a sheet of paper to record your mental pictures. When I am reading today, I will stop along the way and give you a chance to visualize. Then you can transfer this mental image on your paper.* | Activates prior knowledge, thinks about the author's language, and begins to create individual mental images.<br><br><br><br><br><br><br><br>**Student** |
| During<br><br>High<br>↑<br>↓<br>Low | **Teacher**<br>*Before I read, I want you to sketch a picture in the first box showing me what you think of/see when I read the title, The Napping House.*<br><br>Allow time for a quick sketch.<br><br>*I would like you to listen with your eyes closed today. As I read, I want you to create the pictures in your mind.*<br><br>Read the first three pages, stop on page 4 (granny page), and allow students to sketch | Student examples:<br>See Figures 3.3, 3.4, 3.5 |

*(Continued)*

**Table 3.3** (Continued)

| | | |
|---|---|---|
| | what they see in their minds.<br><br>*In the next box, sketch what you are seeing in your mind right now.*<br><br>Continue reading to page 12 (mouse page). *We have lots of new information. I can imagine that your picture has changed greatly. Take a minute to sketch this new mental picture.*<br><br>Read through the last page.<br><br>*Wow! A lot has happened in the last few pages of the story. My mental movie is really playing now! I can hear the snores! I can't wait to see what your mental movie is showing in your mind. Please take a minute to sketch this image in your last box.* | |
| **After**<br>High ↕ Low | Have students meet in small groups to share their mental movies. Take notes on how their images changed or did not change as the story progressed. Finally, assess the students' learning by asking the following questions:<br><br>*How does playing a movie in your mind help you understand a story? Why are our movies sometimes different from one another? What happens to our movies as we gather more information from the story?*<br>**Teacher** | **Student**<br>Actively engages in the small group discussions to share the similarities and differences among sketches. Responds to the teacher's questions to demonstrate understanding of this cognitive strategy. |

**Figure 3.3**

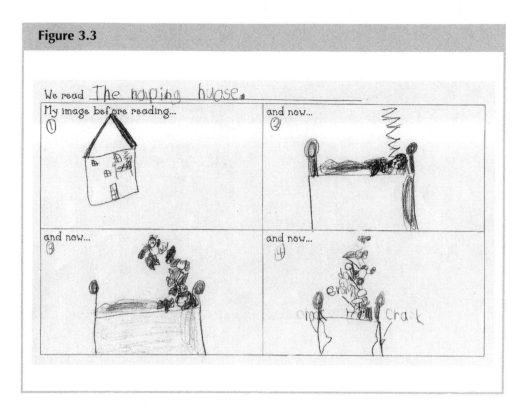

**Figure 3.4**

**Figure 3.5**

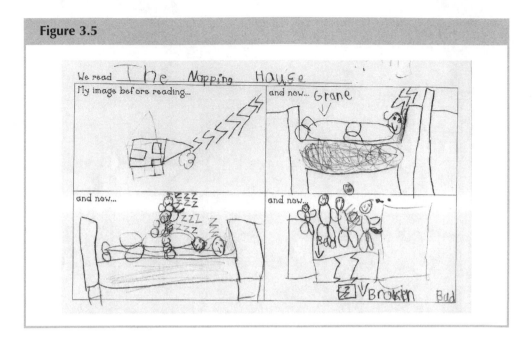

students are excited about literature. Text selection seems to be critical in engaging the students. All of the texts I have used to teach comprehension lessons are placed in a special basket in our classroom library. These are the most popular books. Even after we have spent three or four days reading them, the students never seem to tire of them. In fact, after Day 2 of *The Napping House*, students were begging me to share the pictures with them. When we did share the book the next day, the students were excited to see the illustrator's vision of the story. It led into a great discussion about how everyone's schema is different, which is why our mental pictures are different even though we read the same book!

Meanwhile, in his suburban third grade classroom, Jonathan is busy creating the most optimal learning environment so his students can independently apply their visualization strategies. He chooses to have a variety of books available for students at his listening center including *A Bad Case of Stripes* and *Putting the World to Sleep*. He realizes that all of his students will be able to apply visualization as they listen to these books. He continues to monitor students' behaviors very closely by providing support during this time. Continuously conferencing with his third graders, he realizes that this is a continuous process of revisiting and combining strategy within strategy.

Jonathan shares his thoughts as he coached his students through the initial part of the independent application phase:

I had students stop three times during the reading of the book and draw (using color) the pictures they saw in their minds. Students were attentive and excited to practice visualizing on their own. At the end of the lesson, I had students do a self-evaluation. I showed them pictures from the picture book and asked them to think about how their pictures differed with the real illustrations. I asked them why these differences may occur. They were able to justify their illustrations by sharing the prior knowledge they activated to create their sketches.

I have a few thoughts concerning this lesson and how my students reacted to the visualizing strategy:

*Students were excited about this strategy and wanted to apply the strategy independently.*

*Many students were ready to be released to practice this strategy independently.*

*My students drew more detailed, comprehensive pictures when I was reading a text aloud than when they read a text independently.*

*When students read independently I felt they did not have a conference tool or question to ask themselves to test their visualizing.*

*Last, I felt the self-check at the end of this lesson was helpful for students to monitor their own thinking.*

*Some students may want to visualize, but are simply not prepared with the metacognitive skills.*

I began to have students read independently more often in order to provide the individual instruction each student needed. They were able to keep records of their drawings and thinking within their reading journals.

Finally, after lunch each day, students completed twenty minutes of sustained silent reading. I used this time to conference with them about their text, their thoughts about the text, and how they were using the visualizing strategy. I asked students, "Are you visualizing?" Almost all students would nod their heads "yes." Then I would ask, "How do you know?" Some students would tell me about a running video they were seeing in their heads. Others would stare blankly at me. I would ask those confused students to read a small section for me. They would, and then I would ask what pictures they saw in their minds. Some would be able to give me detailed descriptions; others would give me vague concepts. I find that it is necessary to revisit these strategies independently of one another, yet continue to show students how good readers access all strategies during a reading.

## Table 3.4

**NCTE Standards:**

**1.** Students read a wide range of print and nonprint texts to build an understanding of texts, of themselves, and of the cultures of the United States and the world; to acquire new information; to respond to the needs and demands of society and the workplace; and for personal fulfillment. Among these texts are fiction and nonfiction, classic and contemporary works.

*(Continued)*

**Table 3.4** (Continued)

**3.** Students apply a wide range of strategies to comprehend, interpret, evaluate, and appreciate texts. They draw on their prior experience, their interactions with other readers and writers, their knowledge of word meaning and of other texts, their word identification strategies, and their understanding of textual features (e.g., sound-letter correspondence, sentence structure, context, graphics).

**Picture Book:** Students self-select their text at the listening center. See Resources for suggested titles.

| | | | |
|---|---|---|---|
| **Before** | High ↕ Low | **Teacher** *Remember when we read together_____, _____, _____, and _____ and we shared our mental images for creating our personal movies? As you independently listen to ____ at the listening center, you may want to sketch your mental images. This way, I can see where and what you are visualizing.* | Self-selects a piece of literature to listen to at the listening center. **Student** |
| **During** | High ↕ Low | In between small group instruction and/or during transition time, evaluate the students' use of prior knowledge and visualizing. Make sure prior knowledge is appropriate and the images change as new information is learned. Notice the details of the sketches being shared. You may want to make anecdotal notes for when and for whom this process breaks down. You will use the notes to adjust small group instruction. **Teacher** | Listens to _____ and sketches mental images. **Student** |
| **After** | High ↕ Low | During transition time, ask for volunteers to share their sketches and their thinking. **Teacher** | **Student** Orally shares thinking and sketches. (Sketches may be shared on a Graffiti Door/Wall, or large blank sheet of white paper taped to a door or wall. Students write the title of their story and attach the sketch they created during independent reading.) |

**Figure 3.6**

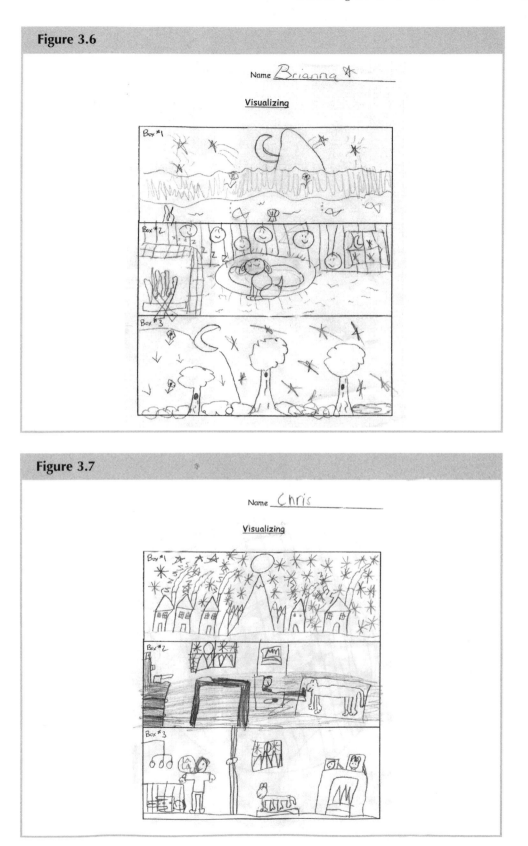

## SUMMARY

- Visualization, as a cognitive strategy, has been shown to be effective with a range of learners.
- Instruction must emphasize the active engagement of the reader in appropriate descriptive texts.
- Visualization enhances not only comprehension, but also enjoyment.
- Students can learn to visualize as an independent strategy in listening, reading, and writing.

Before continuing on your thinking adventure, stop and reflect . . .

**Table 3.5**

| Make your thinking visible . . . | | |
|---|---|---|
| **Reflection Questions:** | *How does the image in my mind extend my thinking? How does deeper meaning help students interact with the author?* | |
| **Modeling Through Think Aloud** — High ↕ Low | **Teacher** | **Student** |
| **Guided Practice** — High ↕ Low | **Teacher** | **Student** |
| **Independent Application** — High ↕ Low | **Teacher** | **Student** |

# 4 Piecing the Clues Together

## *Inferring*

*When the mind is thinking, it is talking to itself.*

—Plato

In Diane's third grade inclusion classroom, we are able to observe an atmosphere of thinkers. Diane has carefully crafted this environment by scaffolding her instruction to develop inferential readers. These eager third graders want to be "in the book!" They want to be that fly on the wall during the dinner scene. They want to solve the characters' problems and give the characters advice.

Thinking while reading is such a powerful strategy that we explicitly teach our young readers. We show them how to draw conclusions as they make connections to their schemata and question their understanding. When readers understand the text beyond the literal level, they imagine they are there. They feel the characters' agony, happiness, and tribulation. They try to solve the problems. The setting comes alive with the noises they hear and the scents in the air.

Take a minute to examine Figure 4.1. What story comes to your mind?

- Why is this person hanging on to this post?
- What is happening?
- How is this person feeling?

**Figure 4.1**

We infer when we tell a story using our prior knowledge and clues from the picture. Inferring is the process of judging, concluding, or reasoning from some given information. It is the heart of meaning construction for learners of all ages (Anderson & Pearson, 1984). Readers are not making random guesses as to the implied meaning; rather, they are systematically thinking about the author's clues and applying it to their schemata (Duffy, 2003).

Inferring is the ability to "read between the lines" or to get the meaning the author implies but does not directly state. We need to teach students that reading is a matter of actively building meaning, based upon prior knowledge and information from the text(s). We can initiate this process by introducing the concept of making inferences using pictures.

As Diane's students enter her third grade inclusion classroom, the students notice a picture illuminated on the overhead from Chris Van Allsburg's *The Mysteries of Harris Burdick*. In this particular sketch, an old sea captain holds a lantern up in the foggy night as he describes the ships coming in and out of the harbor to a young boy by his side. The details of the background intrigue the students.

Immediately, they begin to ask questions:

- Where is this?
- Why is this picture on the screen?
- What is the man doing to the little boy?
- What are they waiting for?

Diane encourages the students to take their seats and create an oral story for the picture. They share their story with peers. The hums of imaginative authors begin to spread throughout the classroom. Their faces light up as their audience listens and adds to their stories. Some students receive applause when sharing their story with the class.

Finally, Bradley asks, "Well, Mrs. Havighurst, what really happened?"

Diane replies, "What do you think happened?"

Bradley shares his inference of what happened.

"I think this is at the Boston Harbor. I think his grandfather is explaining the harbor's functions to his grandson."

Diane asks him why he created this story. He shares his own experiences about his grandfather, who was a sailor, and his visit to the Boston Harbor. Diane tells the class that Bradley inferred; he used clues from the picture to activate his prior knowledge and then drew a conclusion. His conclusion-story is his inference.

Diane continues to share with her students that inferring is a very personal comprehension strategy. "You bring your personal experiences to the text based on clues provided by the author—to read between the lines."

Next, Diane gives each group of students a picture from the same book. Each group has an opportunity to share their individual stories with one another.

In order to show students their metacognition of using clues from the picture and their prior knowledge to make an inference, Diane models how to transfer their thoughts onto a three column chart (Figure 4.2).

Diane refers back to Bradley's example of the Boston Harbor and records his thought process as he shares it with his peers (Figure 4.3).

**Figure 4.2**

| Clues From Picture | + Prior Knowledge | = Inference |
|---|---|---|
|  |  |  |
|  |  |  |
|  |  |  |
|  |  |  |
|  |  |  |
|  |  |  |

**Figure 4.3**

| Clues From Picture | + Prior Knowledge | = Inference |
|---|---|---|
| The pier and the ships | I visited the Boston Harbor when I was in Second Grade. | I think this is at the Boston Harbor. |
| Man in suit holding lantern | My grandfather was a sailor and has a similar uniform. | I think this grandfather is explaining the harbor's functions to his grandson. |

Diane now asks the student groups to revisit their pictures and record their thinking on a new three column chart (Figure 4.2). Diane and I circulate to scaffold the students' thinking. Some students need support in determining how they "just knew." Since we know it is critical for students to be aware of their thinking processes, we encourage them to record their inference first. Then we encourage our readers to work backwards and share the clues they used and their prior knowledge.

The students transform into investigators with this new thinking skill. Their love for this process emanates as they search for discrete clues to form their hypotheses. They continue investigating other sources over the next several days, using pictures from other wordless books, captionless newspaper and magazine pictures, and illustrations from calendars. Students demonstrate their understanding of the metacognitive processes with their completed three columns.

In Table 4.1, we can see how this responsibility for inferring is gradually transferred from teacher to student.

**Table 4.1**

**NCTE Standards:**

**1.** Students read a wide range of print and nonprint texts to build an understanding of texts, of themselves, and of the cultures of the United States and the world; to acquire new information; to respond to the needs and demands of society and the workplace; and for personal fulfillment. Among these texts are fiction and nonfiction, classic and contemporary works.

*(Continued)*

**Table 4.1** (Continued)

**3.** Students apply a wide range of strategies to comprehend, interpret, evaluate, and appreciate texts. They draw on their prior experience, their interactions with other readers and writers, their knowledge of word meaning and of other texts, their word identification strategies, and their understanding of textual features (e.g., sound-letter correspondence, sentence structure, context, graphics).

**Guiding Question**: *How will students be able to connect their prior knowledge with clues from the text in order to develop their inferential thinking?*

| Modeling Through Think Aloud | High ↕ Low | **Teacher** Build an understanding of text and the interrelationships of the readers' background experiences and questions, and the author's clues. | Develops an awareness of activating prior knowledge, asks questions and searches the text for clues. **Student** |
|---|---|---|---|
| Guided Practice | High ↕ Low | Continue to build an understanding of text and the interrelationships of the readers' background experiences and questions, and the author's clues. **Teacher** | Begins to activate prior knowledge, asks questions, and searches the text for clues. **Student** |
| Independent Application | High ↕ Low | Monitor students' activation of prior knowledge, asking questions, and making connections to clues from the text in order to make inferences. **Teacher** | **Student** Activates prior knowledge, asks questions, and searches the text for clues. |

Diane and I decide to use Eve Bunting's *Dandelions* (1995). We believe this text offers multiple opportunities for students to question. Student questions arise from the prior knowledge they learned in social studies about frontier life. They apply this prior knowledge with the clues from the text to infer. See Table 4.2.

**Table 4.2**

| NCTE Standards: |
| --- |
| **1.** Students read a wide range of print and nonprint texts to build an understanding of texts, of themselves, and of the cultures of the United States and the world; to acquire new information; to respond to the needs and demands of society and the workplace; and for personal fulfillment. Among these texts are fiction and nonfiction, classic and contemporary works.<br><br>**3.** Students apply a wide range of strategies to comprehend, interpret, evaluate, and appreciate texts. They draw on their prior experience, their interactions with other readers and writers, their knowledge of word meaning and of other texts, their word identification strategies, and their understanding of textual features (e.g., sound-letter correspondence, sentence structure, context, graphics). |

| **Picture Book:** *Dandelions* by Eve Bunting | | |
| --- | --- | --- |
| | **Teacher** | |
| **Before**<br>High ↕ Low | *Let's examine the front cover of this book.*<br><br>*As a reader what do we notice?*<br><br>*Where do you think these people are going?*<br><br>*Who are these people?*<br><br>*Remember, good readers are good thinkers. Good thinkers use clues from pictures and text and add it to what they already know to make inferences.*<br><br>*Why did you guess that they are pioneers going out west? Let's record this thinking in our three-column chart.*<br>See Figure 4.4. | *The title is* <u>Dandelions</u> *and it was written by Eve Bunting.*<br><br>*They are going out west.*<br>*They are pioneers.*<br><br><br><br><br><br><br><br><br><br>**Student** |
| **During**<br>High ↕ Low | *As I read* <u>Dandelions</u>, *I want to share how I use clues from the book–pictures and text–to make inferences. When I think out loud, I will close the book and record my thinking process on the chart.*<br><br>Begin reading text aloud. Pause at the end of the 4th page.<br>**Teacher** | Listens and observes as teacher reads and thinks aloud.<br><br><br><br><br><br><br><br>**Student** |

*(Continued)*

**Table 4.2** (Continued)

| | | | |
|---|---|---|---|
| | | *I don't think they are going very fast if they only travel 12 miles each day. I drive 10 miles to work each day.*<br><br>Continue reading to the middle of the 9th page.<br><br>*I think Rebecca is scared. My lips quiver when I am scared.*<br><br>Continue reading to the end of the 15th page.<br><br>*I don't like the Svenson boys. They are teasing the girls about mice nesting in their hair and laughing at what they know about constellations.*<br><br>Continue reading to the middle of the 18th page.<br><br>*I think the hole they dug was very deep.* | |
| **After** | High ↕ Low | *As we review my three column chart, we can see I used clues from the text and my prior knowledge to build an understanding of <u>Dandelions</u>.*<br>**Teacher** | **Student**<br>Reviews the three-column chart. |

**Figure 4.4**

| Clues From Picture | + Prior Knowledge | = Inference |
|---|---|---|
| Oxen pulling covered wagon in a field | Pioneers traveled west in covered wagons across prairies | A family of pioneers are going west to settle. |
| 12 miles a day | My trip to work is 10 miles each way | I don't think they are going very far along their journey. |
| Quivered | Once when I was scared, my lips were shaking. My mom said my lips were quivering. | I think Rebecca is scared to live far from the river. |
| "Are you girls afraid of mice…they'll probably nest in your hair." | My brother tries to freak me out with spider stories all the time. | I don't think the Svenson boys want to be friends since they tease the girls. |

| Clues From Picture | + Prior Knowledge | = Inference |
|---|---|---|
| We almost dug ourselves a hole into China! | When we were digging a fire pit in our backyard. My dad told me to stop or else I would end up in China. The hole I dug was over 6 feet deep. | I think they had to dig a very deep hole to find water. |

After our explicit instruction, we feel our students have gathered enough examples to be released into the guided practice phase of instruction. We still want some control, so we continue to read *Dandelions* to the class but invite them to begin recording their own inferences (Table 4.3). Students use the pictures and the words from the text to build their inferences. (See Figure 4.5.)

**Table 4.3**

**NCTE Standards:**

1. Students read a wide range of print and nonprint texts to build an understanding of texts, of themselves, and of the cultures of the United States and the world; to acquire new information; to respond to the needs and demands of society and the workplace; and for personal fulfillment. Among these texts are fiction and nonfiction, classic and contemporary works.

3. Students apply a wide range of strategies to comprehend, interpret, evaluate, and appreciate texts. They draw on their prior experience, their interactions with other readers and writers, their knowledge of word meaning and of other texts, their word identification strategies, and their understanding of textual features (e.g., sound-letter correspondence, sentence structure, context, graphics).

**Picture Book:** *Dandelions* by Eve Bunting

| Before | | Teacher | |
|---|---|---|---|
| | High ↑ ↓ Low | *Remember when I read Dandelions and I shared my thinking? By combining clues from the text and pictures with my prior knowledge, I was able to develop a better understanding of the story and the characters' emotions. You will have an opportunity to record your thinking as I read aloud. You will use clues from the book with your prior knowledge to develop your thinking. Use this chart to record your thoughts. See Figure 4.5.* | **Student** |

*(Continued)*

**Table 4.3** (Continued)

| | | Teacher | Student |
|---|---|---|---|
| During | High ↕ Low | Monitor students' reading behaviors and scaffold their use of book clues and prior knowledge to support their inferences. Provide specific examples when this process breaks down. **Teacher** | Reads the rest (pages 20–44) of *Dandelions* and records the clues, prior knowledge, and inferences. **Student** |
| After | High ↕ Low | Ask for student volunteers to share their three column charts and how their inferences were developed from the prior knowledge and clues from the book. **Teacher** | **Student** Listens to peer responses. |

**Figure 4.5**

| Clues From Picture | + Prior Knowledge | = Inference |
|---|---|---|
| Girls whispering | When I tell a secret I trust that person. | I think sisters really trust each other. |
| Girls digging and the word "drooped" | I planted droopy marigolds in the dirt and they died. | I think dandelions will die and their mother will be sad. |
| Family hugging and the words, "Mama gave a shaky little sigh." | Hugs make me happy when I am scared. | Mama will feel better because she got hugged. |

Finally, after this phase of differentiated instruction, most students are ready to be released into the independent application phase. They thoroughly enjoy being able to make their thinking visible with their three column charts.

**Table 4.4**

| NCTE Standards: |
| --- |
| **1.** Students read a wide range of print and nonprint texts to build an understanding of texts, of themselves, and of the cultures of the United States and the world; to acquire new information; to respond to the needs and demands of society and the workplace; and for personal fulfillment. Among these texts are fiction and nonfiction, classic and contemporary works.<br><br>**3.** Students apply a wide range of strategies to comprehend, interpret, evaluate, and appreciate texts. They draw on their prior experience, their interactions with other readers and writers, their knowledge of word meaning and of other texts, their word identification strategies, and their understanding of textual features (e.g., sound-letter correspondence, sentence structure, context, graphics). |

| | | |
| --- | --- | --- |
| Picture Book: *Dandelions* by Eve Bunting | | |
| **Before**<br>High ↕ Low | **Teacher**<br>*Remember when you used clues from the book and your prior knowledge to explain your thinking? As you independently read _____ back at your seat, you may use another three column chart to record your thinking.* | Self-selects a piece of literature at independent level.<br><br><br><br><br>**Student** |
| **During**<br>High ↕ Low | In between small group instruction and/or during transition time, evaluate students' inferences. Make sure clues from the book and prior knowledge are being used to enhance their understanding as they make inferences. Make anecdotal notes when and for whom this process breaks down. Use the notes to adjust small group instruction.<br>**Teacher** | Reads _____ and records the clues from the book that have been combined with prior knowledge to make inferences.<br><br><br><br><br>**Student** |
| **After**<br>High ↕ Low | Ask for student volunteers to share their three column charts and how their final inferences enhanced their understanding.<br>**Teacher** | **Student**<br>Listens to peer responses. |

We model inferring as an intriguing comprehension strategy. We make this abstract concept concrete by selecting pictures portraying familiar concepts. Students realize inferring will differ among themselves.

## SUMMARY

- When readers read meaningful texts which offer opportunities to infer, they learn to infer.
- When readers infer, they use their prior knowledge with textual information to develop their thoughts.
- When readers infer, they elaborate upon what they read to draw conclusions.
- When readers infer, they personalize what they read to build a deeper meaning.

Before continuing on your thinking adventure, stop and reflect . . .

**Table 4.5**

| Make your thinking visible . . . | | |
|---|---|---|
| **Reflection Questions:** | *How does piecing clues together help me infer? How does inferring help my students bring deeper meaning to the text?* | |
| **Modeling Through Think Aloud**  High ↕ Low | **Teacher**<br><br><br><br><br>**Student** | |
| **Guided Practice**  High ↕ Low | **Teacher** | **Student** |
| **Independent Application**  High ↕ Low | **Student**<br><br><br><br>**Teacher** | |

# 5 Sifting Through and Locating the Nugget

## *Determining Importance*

*Information overload is the inability to extract needed knowledge from an immense quantity of information.*

—Mark R. Nelson

It is 7:00 A.M., two hours before students arrive, and there is a small group of us meeting to share our thoughts, ideas, and new findings on how to teach our students to actively read nonfiction text.

After reading the works of Stephanie Harvey and Anne Goudvis (2000), Debbie Miller (2002), Linda Hoyt (2005), and Richard Vacca (2002) we come to the conclusion that, as teachers, our primary responsibility in teaching nonfiction texts is to help students understand the importance of text features, and how they can help or hinder the reader. We must model for students how these features support the subject matter or cause confusion, how these features help define what to read and in what order, and how the features help identify the author's intended message. All of these skills are critical for students to confirm or readjust their prior knowledge.

Helping children determine what is important in reading, writing, and other content areas is our sole purpose for teaching. We want them to make connections by sifting, sorting, and eliminating old or incorrect information with newly learned information. By asking questions, synthesizing, visualizing, and inferring students can determine what information deserves the most attention.

Working with Alicia's third graders, I notice many of her students demonstrate knowledge with text features. As readers, they are beginning to set their own purposes for reading by answering a question and confirming their own prior knowledge. They decide what is essential. However, sometimes students don't have the opportunity to set their own purposes. The purpose is set by others. It may be the classroom teacher; it may be the author's purpose in writing the text; or, it may be the genre's purpose. By genre, I am referring to standardized state tests. As Alicia's students are beginning to find out, they need to know who has identified their purposes for reading and how their prior knowledge can help or hinder their understandings. Who is most important: the reader, the author, or the test?

To help students decide who is important and who is controlling their purpose in reading, I distribute handouts of a picture of a house. The house is also displayed on the overhead.

As the children are each given a picture of the house, I ask them to identify what they think is the most important part of the house by circling or outlining the specific area. As I circulate through the classroom, I notice many have circled the door, some the roof, and a couple of students have outlined the outside lines to the house. Calling on one student at a time, I hand over the overhead pen and invite each to share his or her thinking.

**Figure 5.1**

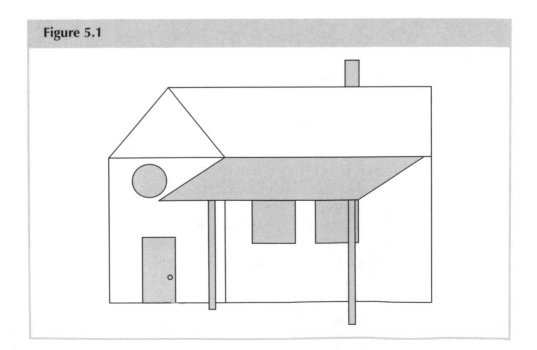

The students who chose the roof articulate their reasons. Many discuss the importance of protection from weather related incidents. Those who chose the door believe that is the easiest way to enter the house, rather than through a window. Those who outlined the outside lines share how the frame of the house holds everything together. Through their answers we can see each student took a different perspective based upon prior knowledge and individual purpose.

## IMPORTANCE BASED UPON PURPOSE

Next, I tell the class, let's take a different twist. Suppose I told you that I am the architect of this house. I am the person who designed the structure and the features of the house. After this announcement, I provide some background information, telling them that this house is located in Florida. The house faces west. This means that in the heat of the day or the hottest part of the day, the sun is shining on the front of the house. Now I ask the same question, what do you think is the most important part of the house? Again, walking around, I notice everyone has circled the awning. Asking why they circled the awning, everyone shares the same reason—to protect the house from the heat so the sun doesn't shine into the windows. Debriefing, we share how these two different purposes define different answers. In the first picture of the house, they set the purpose, but in the second picture of the house, as the architect, I set the purpose. Like the architect, authors do the same thing. They have their own purposes for writing, and it may be different from the students'. As good readers, before we begin to read, we need to identify who is setting the purpose. When students are negotiating through a variety of text or genres, students need to know who is setting the purpose and who is important. Is it the reader or the author?

Entering Alicia's room, I hear her review the table of contents chart she is using with her students. The purpose of this chart is to help students see how a table of contents can help them easily locate information and continuously activate their schemata. Before reading, students complete the first column of the chart by identifying the section or chapter title and then make a prediction about the contents of the chapter. In the second column, students brainstorm words they think will appear throughout the chapter. After reading, students complete the third column and share key words or ideas.

On their class chart, in the first column, they have the section title, "Where Fish Live." By sharing their prior knowledge, they decided that the author would use words such as "ocean," "pond," "lake," and "underwater" to describe where fish live. When Alicia finishes reading, they discover fish also live in mudflats, rivers, streams, and coral reefs. Alicia references their table of contents chart, highlighting the differences between the conceptual words in column two and the specific vocabulary learned while reading. Here Alicia points out how chapter titles are the umbrella for learned information.

Together the students decide the vocabulary falls under the umbrella of the chapter title, "Where Fish Live," which also provides the frame for learned information.

Today, the students continue with their table of contents chart, focusing on the parts of the fish. Their responses indicate how this section triggers words like "gills," "fins," and "eyes."

After Alicia finishes her shared Think Aloud with her students, I have some of her students join me at the back table for a guided reading lesson. As I observe these students during their shared Think Alouds and previous guided reading lessons, I know these students listen intently; they interact, ask questions, and engage with their fellow classmates. I also notice that on their anchor chart they have listed other text features, and how these features help with identifying key elements within the text.

Alicia's students can decode text easily; they have lots of experiences with different types of text, and through their conversations they share many of these worldly experiences. They also ask thoughtful questions, showing how they can monitor their own reading. Thinking about these students, their reading behaviors, and our curriculum, I purposely select a text that has few features. This text is filled with beautiful photographs of coral reefs, fish, and other inhabitants. Most of the text has a full two page spread with these pictures inserted at the bottom of the pages. Under the pictures are captions to help define the author's intent. This text is inconsiderate because of the visual stimulation, the limited text features, and the photographs embedded within. I think many nonfiction texts are designed and written for adults because we select and purchase the text for our students. However, students need to be exposed to considerate text, or text that includes many text features to support the organizational structures

**Table 5.1** Table-of-Contents Predictions

| Before-Reading Content Predictions | Before-Reading Word Predictions | After-Reading Reflections |
|---|---|---|
| What do I think I will learn? | Name specific words you think will appear. | What are the key words and ideas? |
| Chapter: Where Fish Live, p. 12 | Oceans, ponds, lakes, underwater | Mudflats, rivers, streams, coral reefs |
| Chapter: Parts on a fish's body, p. 20 | Gills, fins, scales, eye color, heart | |
| Chapter: | | |

**Figure 5.2**

**Table-of-Contents Predictions**

| Before-Reading Content Predictions | Before-Reading Word Predictions | After-Reading Reflections |
|---|---|---|
| What do I think I will learn? | Name specific words you think will appear. | Key words and ideas |
| Chapter: Where Fish Live, p. 12 | Oceans, ponds, lakes, underwater | Mudflats, rivers, streams, coral reefs |
| Chapter: Parts on a fish's body, p. 20 | Gills, fins, scales, eye color, heart | |
| Chapter: | | |

and functions of the author's message and/or the child's background experiences.

Students need to be exposed to considerate text before interacting with inconsiderate text, which hinders their comprehension.

Linking Alicia's explicit instruction on text features with the students' prior knowledge, and having them define their own purposes, sets the stage for their guided reading lesson. Now, word choice is critical. Students need to hear and see how the shared Think Aloud links to their guided reading lesson. Sometimes they need to visually see it.

**Figure 5.3    This Is What We Already Know About Nonfiction Text**

| Page Number | Text Feature | Text/Reasons |
|---|---|---|
| Pages 14–15 | Title: Coral Reefs in Danger | |
| | map | Correlates the reefs in danger to the ones that are not in danger |
| Page 8 | bold print | fish/parts |
| Page 6 | labels | |
| | labels | different kinds of sponges |

(Text Continues on Page 92)

**Table 5.2**

<table>
<tr><td colspan="3">

**NCTE Standards:**

**1.** Students read a wide range of print and nonprint texts to build an understanding of texts, of themselves, and of the cultures of the United States and the world; to acquire new information; to respond to the needs and demands of society and the workplace; and for personal fulfillment. Among these texts are fiction and nonfiction, classic and contemporary works.

**3.** Students apply a wide range of strategies to comprehend, interpret, evaluate, and appreciate texts. They draw on their prior experience, their interactions with other readers and writers, their knowledge of word meaning and of other texts, their word identification strategies, and their understanding of textual features (e.g., sound-letter correspondence, sentence structure, context, graphics).

</td></tr>
<tr><td colspan="3">

**Informational Text:** *Dive! My Adventure in the Deep Frontier* by Sylvia A. Earle

</td></tr>
<tr>
<td>**Modeling Through Think Aloud**<br><br>High ↑ ↓ Low</td>
<td>

**Teacher**

*When reading nonfiction text, we know the author uses many text features to help us quickly and efficiently determine important information. The book I am sharing today is <u>Dive! My Adventure in the Deep Frontier</u> by Sylvia A. Earle. As you know I am very interested in coral reefs. We know when we want to find specific information; we use the table of contents or the index. Let's take a look and see which will help us find information about coral reefs.*

</td>
<td>

Students will be looking at the front cover of the book as I introduce our purpose and plan.




**Student**

</td>
</tr>
<tr>
<td>**Guided Practice**<br><br>High ↑ ↓ Low</td>
<td>

*When I want to find specific information quickly, I go to the index first. The index is in alphabetical order; it is detailed and it will tell us how much information the author has written about a specific item. Let's look at the top of the page because there is some information about the index. (Point to the top of the page and read.)*

*Now we know if the page numbers are bold, we will find*

</td>
<td>

Students are looking at an overhead copy of the index.

Students are looking at an overhead copy of the table of contents.




**Student**

</td>
</tr>
</table>

| | | |
|---|---|---|
| | *illustrations about the topic and if not we will find the author's written information. We know coral reefs begin with a "c" and as we scan down the page we find coral reefs. We find many bolded page numbers and more specific information about coral reefs. There are two pages about the diseases of the reefs, and reef-building plants. Notice how quickly we found this information. Now let's look at the table of contents.* (Read overhead of table of contents, pointing to each chapter.)<br><br>*By reading these headings, I cannot be sure if I will find specific information about coral reefs. We see the author has sequenced her dive by the chapter headings and not by ocean life.*<br><br>*Now as the reader, I realize the index will help me more. And I have to decide if I want to look at the illustrations first or read about diseases or plant life in the coral reefs.*<br><br>**Teacher** | |
| Independent Application<br><br>High ↕ Low | *Today we looked at the table of contents and the index. We learned the index provides us with a more efficient way of finding specific information quickly. We also learned how broad the titles are within the table of contents and how the table of contents could sequence the author's story or information. As you meet in your guided reading groups I want you to bring this thinking along with you about the index and table of contents. We will add this to our anchor chart.* (Have a student state in his/her own words the purpose of the index and table of contents.)<br><br>**Teacher** | **Student**<br>Students turn and share with a partner the purpose of the index. Have one or two students report out. Chart.<br><br>Students turn and share with a partner the purpose of the table of contents. Have one or two students report out. Chart. |

**Table 5.3**

| | | Teacher | Students are referencing |
|---|---|---|---|

**NCTE Standards:**

**1.** Students read a wide range of print and nonprint texts to build an understanding of texts, of themselves, and of the cultures of the United States and the world; to acquire new information; to respond to the needs and demands of society and the workplace; and for personal fulfillment. Among these texts are fiction and nonfiction, classic and contemporary works.

**3.** Students apply a wide range of strategies to comprehend, interpret, evaluate, and appreciate texts. They draw on their prior experience, their interactions with other readers and writers, their knowledge of word meaning and of other texts, their word identification strategies, and their understanding of textual features (e.g., sound-letter correspondence, sentence structure, context, graphics).

**Guiding Question:** *What are the features of informational text and how do they help me interpret the text?*

| Before Reading | High ↕ Low | **Teacher** *As I listened to Mrs. Granger explain the purpose of the table of contents and how it helps us locate information, I also noticed on your Anchor Chart some of the other text features you've been discussing such as captions, photographs, pictures, bold print, italic print, and titles. And as you noted, all of these features help you define what is important. In the text we are previewing and reading today, there are some sections which seem to be more considerate than others. As a reader some text can be considerate because specific features are used to help locate important information. When a text is inconsiderate, you may not have enough prior knowledge or the author chose to eliminate some text features. By previewing the text at your seat, I noticed on your chart, you have gathered some information about the destruction of coral reefs. By using the table of contents let's turn to pages 14–15 to learn about the coral reefs in danger. As we look at this page, we notice there are few text features. Because of the bright* | Students are referencing back to their previous lessons on text features and their prior knowledge. They are also following along as I specifically point out the features on pages 14 and 15. <br><br> **Student** |
|---|---|---|---|

| | | | |
|---|---|---|---|
| | | *red borders, my eyes are immediately drawn to the inserted photos and captions at the bottom of the page rather than the print on the top. Looking at page 14 there are no other text features to help me. Perhaps if the author chose to insert a title or subtitle at the top of the page it may have helped me identify where to begin to read. Now as you read these two pages, I want you to think about why coral reefs are being destroyed and if a text feature would help you determine importance.* | |
| **During Reading Coaching** | High ↕ Low | As students finish reading, provide them with a Post-it note and listen to their selection of the text feature and how it helps clarify their meaning of the text. While noting student's selection, determine if he/she is able to determine importance at the word level, or at the sentence level, or at the text level. Which text feature supports his/her understanding? Coach for clarification how? **Teacher** | Students are reading silently to themselves pages 14–15, noting with a Post-it what text feature would help them comprehend (distinguish important details) the text feature and why. **Student** |
| **After Reading Debriefing** | High ↕ Low | *Now that you have finished reading pages 14–15, how about if we have one student identify the text feature he/she chose and why.* *Let's return to our guided question: What are the features of informational text and how do they help me interpret the text? You stated that bold print would help identify the importance of the word and help you understand the importance of keeping these polyps alive. We will add this new information to our chart. For independent practice, I want you to read pages 6–13 and select a text feature that will help you understand the important details.* **Teacher** | **Student** Student identifies how bolding the important word "polyps" would help him know how this is important to the underwater food chain. Student also debriefs how he needed to reread to identify a single word, "polyps," rather than bolding the entire sentence. |

## DETERMINING IMPORTANCE
## DURING GUIDED READING

The guided practice, the We Do phase, is the heart and soul. It provides you, as the teacher, with pertinent information about your students and yourself as the teacher. Did they understand the purpose of the lesson? Was the text too difficult? Were the students active readers (questioning, predicting, reflecting, synthesizing, summarizing, self-monitoring)? What will be the next teaching points? This guided reading lesson is connected to, and built upon, the shared Think Aloud from previous days, the students' prior knowledge, and their reading and writing behaviors.

By observing the students' behaviors and listening to their conversations during their guided reading lesson, I realize there are some students ready to move on and others who are not sure about some of the features' purposes. One student bolds an entire sentence rather than a specific word, whereas another student thinks a subtitle benefits the reader by helping identify the author's intent or purpose. She also thinks the subtitle helps the reader navigate through the page or as she states, "It tells me where I should begin to read." Another student wants to add a map. He thinks a map would help compare and contrast the difference between endangered coral reefs and those surviving reefs.

During the next guided reading group, I observe that the reading behaviors are entirely different. During the shared Think Alouds, they listen but not as intently; their interactions with the text and with their fellow classmates are superficial, and they very rarely ask clarifying questions. I also know from listening to their previous guided reading groups that they still have difficulty decoding multisyllabic words; they have difficulty self-monitoring their reading behaviors, and they have limited skills to help them become independent readers.

Again, building upon Alicia's shared Think Aloud from her We Do phase, the guiding question remains the same. However, this group's text has different challenges. I note some challenging words for the group, "plunging" and "aquariums," because this group has difficulty decoding multisyllabic words. I also wonder if these words are in their speaking vocabularies. If not, then the students will have the added challenge of not only decoding, but also comprehending, at the word level. Just like the previous group's text, this text also has pictures at the bottom of the page.

On the previous day, I had them chart what they thought they knew about whales. (See Figure 5.5.) This variation of Donna Ogle's Know, Want to know, Learn (KWL) by Tony Stead (2005) is in his book *Reality Checks: Teaching Reading Comprehension with Non-Fiction K–5*. In the first column he has students identify what they think they know about a specific topic. In the next column they confirm their prior knowledge, rather than continuing

**Table 5.4**

<table>
<tr><td colspan="3">

**NCTE Standards:**

**1.** Students read a wide range of print and nonprint texts to build an understanding of texts, of themselves, and of the cultures of the United States and the world; to acquire new information; to respond to the needs and demands of society and the workplace; and for personal fulfillment. Among these texts are fiction and nonfiction, classic and contemporary works.

**3.** Students apply a wide range of strategies to comprehend, interpret, evaluate, and appreciate texts. They draw on their prior experience, their interactions with other readers and writers, their knowledge of word meaning and of other texts, their word identification strategies, and their understanding of textual features (e.g., sound-letter correspondence, sentence structure, context, graphics).

</td></tr>
<tr><td colspan="3">

**Guiding Question:** *What are the features of informational texts and how do they help me interpret the text?*

</td></tr>
</table>

| Before Reading | High ↕ Low | **Teacher** *As I listened to Mrs. Granger explain the purpose of the table of contents and how it helps us locate information, I also noticed on your Anchor Chart some of the other text features you've been discussing such as captions, photographs, pictures, bold print, index, italic print, and titles. And as you noted, all of these features help you define what is important. By using the captions, index, and table of contents, we will be able to help determine if our prior knowledge is accurate. Also, your chart has set the purpose. I notice you stated some information about the whales' diet. Let's turn to the back of the book and look at the index. Scan with your eyes and see if you can locate anything that will help us. If we look at the second column, about three quarters of the way down, we see the word "food." There are several pages which will give us information about the whales' diet. Let's begin with* | Students are focused on the chart and listening for specific instruction. Students are scanning the page locating the word, "food." |

*(Continued)*

**Table 5.4** (Continued)

| | | Teacher | Student |
|---|---|---|---|
| | | *pages 4 and 5 to help us check our prior knowledge.*<br><br>Have students read these two pages and on a Post-it note have them write what whales eat. | |
| **Guided Practice** | High<br>↕<br>Low | Listening to one student whisper read you want to notice his/her ability to process the text. (What are some challenge words for the student? Does the student demonstrate any independent behaviors: rereading, questioning, thinking about his/her purpose for reading?)<br><br>Provide coaching to problem solve specific words and note behaviors.<br><br>**Teacher** | One student whisper reads, while the other students read silently to themselves.<br><br>As students finish reading, they write their information on the Post-it notes.<br><br>**Student** |
| **After Reading** | High<br>↕<br>Low | *Referencing back to our chart, you only have the word "fish" listed. What did you find out about whales and their diet?*<br><br>In the confirming column, we add "squid," "penguins," and "seals." In addition, I share what reading behaviors the student demonstrated to problem solve the word "plunging." This leads to a quick discussion of the word's meaning.<br><br>*Let's look at our guiding question, What are text features and how do they help interpret facts? What did we find out?*<br><br>*Also, our own purpose for reading led us to determine what was important.*<br><br>**Teacher** | **Student**<br>Acknowledging their chart, students all share the information on their Post-it notes.<br><br>Students shared how the index helped them find specific information about the whales' diet. They also state how the captions provided information about the squids and penguins. |

**Figure 5.4**

---

**This Is What We Already Know About Nonfiction Text**

- **An event that actually happened**
- **Information about a topic**
- **Has photos that are real**
- **Captions (what the pictures are about)**
- **We read to learn more**
- **We can learn about the past**
- **We want to learn more about things we like**

---

on through the text with misinformation. This encompasses the third column, misconceptions. In the fourth column, a word is defined for new information, and the final column includes wonderings. This strategy is called Reading for Analyzing Nonfiction (RAN). Focusing on the first two columns will be our purpose for reading, acknowledging students' prior knowledge as being significant and accurate.

Being aware of students' reading behaviors by listening to one student whisper and read, helping him to problem solve the word "plunging," and overhearing the other students' conversations, the writer of this text had some challenges. Just as the one student has difficulty with the word "plunging," many others struggle as well. "Guzzles" also causes some difficulty. Knowing these words help create a visual image of the whale and its behavior, I decide to explicitly share and model by explaining how Bradley problem solved the word "plunging" and how we can decode "guzzles" and develop word meaning. Also, knowing and understanding these two words will help develop students' speaking and writing vocabularies.

## REVISITING TEXTS

As the students head back to their seats, I realize the importance of previewing the text. When determining importance we look for vocabulary that will enhance understanding, support the purpose for reading, and note the text features that will support or interfere with comprehension. We also need to identify the text structure to help identify language features

**Table 5.5**

| NCTE Standards: |
| --- |
| **1.** Students read a wide range of print and nonprint texts to build an understanding of texts, of themselves, and of the cultures of the United States and the world; to acquire new information; to respond to the needs and demands of society and the workplace; and for personal fulfillment. Among these texts are fiction and nonfiction, classic and contemporary works.<br><br>**3.** Students apply a wide range of strategies to comprehend, interpret, evaluate, and appreciate texts. They draw on their prior experience, their interactions with other readers and writers, their knowledge of word meaning and of other texts, their word identification strategies, and their understanding of textual features (e.g., sound-letter correspondence, sentence structure, context, graphics). |

| **Picture Book:** Students self-select their text. See Resources for suggested titles. | | |
| --- | --- | --- |
| **Before**<br>High ↕ Low | **Teacher**<br>*Remember when we read together _____, _____, _____, and _____ and we shared our text features with one another. As you independently read _____, you will identify which text feature helped or hindered your comprehension.* | Students have self-selected informational text to read.<br><br>**Student** |
| **During**<br>High ↕ Low | In between small group instruction and/or during transition time, evaluate the students' use of text features. Have students verbalize their justification for their text feature selection. You may want to make anecdotal notes for when and whom this process breaks down. You will use the notes to adjust small group instruction.<br>**Teacher** | Students read _____ and record their use of text features.<br><br><br><br><br><br><br>**Student** |
| **After**<br>High ↕ Low | During transition time, ask for volunteers to share their application of text features.<br><br>**Teacher** | **Student**<br>Orally sharing their thinking, they identify the text feature and how it helped or hindered their comprehension. |

presented by the author. We need to share how two vocabulary words like "plunging" and "guzzles" describe the behaviors of the whales. If children are presented with more and more opportunities to hear nonfiction presented along with teachers' shared thinking while they gather specific information, they will begin to understand the multiple structures authors use.

When Alicia's students are ready to learn about text structures, she can revisit the text she has used in her shared Think Aloud. Revisiting text multiple times helps students free up brain space. Students understand the features and some of the content, so they can now concentrate on the structures of the text without having to learn new content information.

**Figure 5.5**

| What do I think I know? | Confirm: Yes, I am right! |
|---|---|
| • sharp teeth | • toothed: 2–200 teeth |
| • big | • squid, seals, penguins (plankton) |
| • eat fish | |
| • live in ocean | |
| • people look at whales | |
| • large mouth, teeth | |
| • huge fin | |
| • some are harmless | |
| • eyes on side | |
| • make sounds when mad | |
| • swallow water | |
| • blow hole | |

Alicia tells students, "Today, we are going to free up brain space by revisiting a text for a different purpose. When learning something new, this is all we want to concentrate on. We already understand the features of the text and how these features helped us learn information about fish. Our purpose today is to listen to the chapter, 'Parts of a Fish,' for specific vocabulary the author uses to describe the fish. Authors use multiple structures when writing nonfiction. Today we are going to explore one structure, the describing structure." Explicitly teaching students the structures helps them find and locate specific information related to their questions.

To build an effective guided reading lesson using the gradual release of responsibility, teachers must always refer back to the known (the child, the text, and the previous day's lessons). What can the students do today that I can build upon tomorrow (Vygotsky, 1978)? Critically observing and coaching students during their guided reading lessons will be the key to moving them forward in determining importance.

As stated in the beginning of the chapter, we need to make sure our students have the capacity to think critically, to integrate or synthesize information, to reorganize their knowledge and/or dismantle misinformation. Helping students to discern information, or determine what is important, is critical because today's information is immediate, fast, and accurate. With so much available information (important, trivial, or entertaining), we must teach our students to determine what is essential (Keene & Zimmerman, 1997).

## SUMMARY

Determining importance is dependent upon the purpose for reading, whether it is the author's purpose or the reader's purpose.

- Determining importance happens at the word level, sentence level, or text level.
- Students need to be taught the importance of text features and structures.
- Text selection is critical when helping students determine importance.
- Determining importance is recursive—recursive in reorganizing our prior knowledge, recursive in analyzing, and recursive in synthesizing this new information.

Before continuing on your thinking adventure, stop and reflect . . .

**Table 5.6**

| Make your thinking visible . . . | | |
|---|---|---|
| **Reflection Questions:** | *What did I learn about the importance of purpose?* | *How does determining importance help my students organize their thinking?* |
| **Modeling Through Think Aloud** High ↕ Low | **Teacher** | **Student** |
| **Guided Practice** High ↕ Low | **Teacher** | **Student** |
| **Independent Application** High ↕ Low | **Teacher** | **Student** |

# 6 Organizing and Re-Creating New Ideas

## Synthesizing

*A mind stretched to a new idea never goes back to its original dimensions.*

—Oliver Wendell Holmes

As I enter Jenn's fifth grade inclusion reading class, I notice groups of students huddled together dumping construction paper shapes in the middle of their tables. Each packet includes one large piece of construction paper, one circle, five triangles, seven squares, and one rectangle of various sizes and colors.

Jenn directs her students, "After I am finished explaining the directions, I want all of you to work in your table groups and combine the shapes I have provided into a picture. Secure the shapes onto the large white piece of construction paper using the scotch tape. There is no correct way to combine the shapes. I want you all to work together in your cooperative groups, not looking at any of the other groups' ideas. You have five minutes to complete this assignment. Good luck!"

Moving around the room, Jenn observes the various pictures created by the children. Using her anecdotal folder, she records their conversations noting how they describe the image to one another. Next she notes how they justify their mental images, and how they articulate the movement of the shapes.

"Okay, time's up! Please select one member from your group to display the picture on the chalkboard."

## STUDENT GROUP A

**Figure 6.1**   This is a picture of our table group. Each of us is sitting at the four corners of the table and the person at the lower right has scissors. There are books out on our desks. Next to our table are the teacher's desk and her work on it.

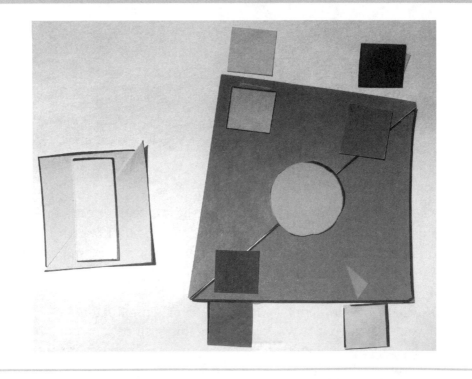

## STUDENT GROUP B

**Figure 6.2**  This is a picture of mountains with the sun rising behind them. There are blue clouds in the sky and green grasses growing on the mountains.

## STUDENT GROUP C

**Figure 6.3**  This is a picture of a clown eating ice cream. He has two blue eyes, two yellow ears, blushed cheeks, and a big black and yellow nose. He is sticking his pink tongue out while eating ice cream.

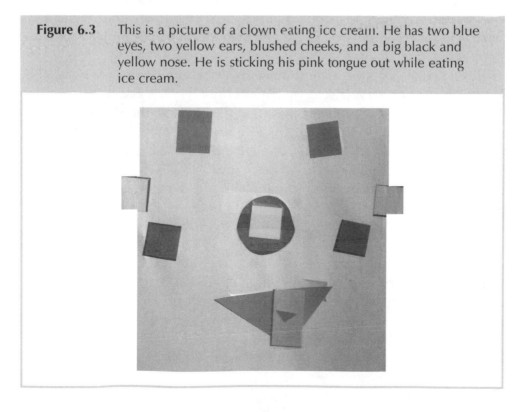

After the groups share their art, Jenn continues her lesson:

> Notice how all the pictures are different, even though we all started
> and used the same shapes. Each picture is different because you
> shared your experiences, justified why your image is important
> and described how to construct it. Each of you has a different way
> of thinking. This is okay! We all put the pieces together, and conse-
> quently we have six unique images.

Jenn knows that students who are good synthesizers bring together
information. She teaches them to use their prior knowledge to build their
schemata to organize their thinking. She then models the process of her
schema changing over time when reading new information. She succeeds
at developing the abstract process of synthesizing, combining elements,
and integrating them into a new whole (Cooper & Kiger, 2006).

Readers need to see the relationships between ideas and expand their
personal understanding. Ultimately, we want readers to realize the big
idea in a text and connect this to a theme in their lives (Fountas & Pinnell,
2001). When readers synthesize, they begin by activating their prior knowledge and then continue to add new information. The proficient reader
then blends the old with the new information. Using the newly blended
information, the reader forms a new idea. A proficient reader continues
this process until reaching the end of the text. The reader now reflects
how schema changes to form a synthesis. At this point, the reader has
constructed a meaning that is greater than the reader's initial thoughts
(Cooper & Kiger, 2006).

Ellin Keene captures synthesizing in yet another concrete way, the
mind's mosaic artistry (Keene & Zimmerman, 1997). She continues to
include within the definition of this cognitive process the skills of order-
ing, recalling, retelling, and recreating. Synthesis is about organizing the
different pieces to create a mosaic, or a meaning and a beauty, greater than
the sum of each shiny piece. We do this in our daily lives. For instance, we
might provide a synthesis of our daily activities when we engage in our
family dinner conversations. My oldest son no longer asks, "Daddy, what
did you build today?" But rather, "Daddy how was your day?" My
husband recalls the day's events and orders them in his retelling as he
recreates the events in a most entertaining way. In the classroom, we nur-
ture this complex process by responding to a similar curiosity of our beginning readers. Transferring the oral retelling to a more active reading
process allows the child to have a concrete understanding of synthesizing.

Realizing the influence text elements have on the readers' evolving syntheses, in another primary classroom, Richard and Basil create an organizer to

**Table 6.1**

| NCTE Standards: |
| --- |
| **1.** Students read a wide range of print and nonprint texts to build an understanding of texts, of themselves, and of the cultures of the United States and the world; to acquire new information; to respond to the needs and demands of society and the workplace; and for personal fulfillment. Among these texts are fiction and nonfiction, classic and contemporary works. |
| **3.** Students apply a wide range of strategies to comprehend, interpret, evaluate, and appreciate texts. They draw on their prior experience, their interactions with other readers and writers, their knowledge of word meaning and of other texts, their word identification strategies, and their understanding of textual features (e.g., sound-letter correspondence, sentence structure, context, graphics). |

*Guiding Question*: *How will students be able to apply their cognitive strategies to create a synthesis?*

| | | |
| --- | --- | --- |
| **Modeling Through Think Aloud** High ↕ Low | **Teacher** Build an understanding of the integration between the reader's background experiences and the text meaning to create a synthesis. | Develops an awareness of the importance of synthesizing information. **Student** |
| **Guided Practice** High ↕ Low | Continue to build an understanding of the integration between the reader's background experiences and the text meaning to create a synthesis. **Teacher** | Begins to integrate prior knowledge and text meaning to create an evolving synthesis. **Student** |
| **Independent Application** High ↕ Low | Monitor students' understanding of the integration between the reader's background experiences and the text meaning to create a synthesis. **Teacher** | **Student** Integrates prior knowledge and text meaning to create an evolving synthesis. |

scaffold more than one reader's thoughts into a logical synthesis. Modeling together in the same sixth grade classroom, they provide explicit instruction.

Using the puzzle organizer Richard and Basil begin to model the processes of activating their prior knowledge. Moving into explicit instruction, Basil begins to read aloud to Richard and the class. After learning story elements, Richard and Basil record the details on their own organizers. Continuing this process of reading, thinking, and recording, they give the students an opportunity to observe how to be an active reader. This process scaffolds the development of their syntheses. (See Figure 6.4.)

After reading the selected text, Richard and Basil demonstrate how to synthesize more than one reader's thoughts. Cutting their puzzle pieces apart, they mix the pieces together. Basil picks a piece out of the pile and notices it is Richard's. Richard reads his notes and elaborates on his thinking. They continue this process, laying the puzzle pieces in front of the class, to construct one puzzle.

Finally, after the fifth day, Jenn's class completes the text. They are ready to discuss their final thoughts—the author's purpose. They discuss their individual ideas, then reflect, and finally record their new thoughts, their syntheses.

Readers are able to synthesize multiple viewpoints during group discussions. It is very critical that readers take the time to share their ideas, reflect, and record. Now, with their newly formed puzzles, readers are ready to share their synthesized thoughts.

When our readers are aware of the evolution of the text's meaning, they create new ways of thinking and share these new insights later. Consequently, they are able to remember the meaning and transfer this information to a new situation.

As we continue to scaffold our comprehension instruction, it is critical to remember that there are many ways of coming to understandings. Some learners need to talk to think. Some learners need to reflect to think. Some learners need to sketch to think. Some learners need to move to think. Some learners need to see to learn. Some learners need to show to learn. We need to meet the needs of all learners. We need to move learners toward synthesizing what they know; the transmediation of information can make a difference (Hoyt, 2005). Transmediation is a process of moving information from one communication system to another (Short, Harste, & Burke, 1996).

In order to provide optimal synthesizing learning environments, we need to promote the transmediation of themes from one text to personal experiences, and then to other texts. We need to scaffold students' learning so they detect the larger meanings which lie below the surface. In order to encourage the growth of their syntheses, we need to ask students to pause after reading a section and discuss what they have noticed, as we prompt them to reveal the overall theme.

As Richard's second graders engage in a conversation about *Yang the Youngest and His Terrible Ear*, their latest read aloud, many students feel

**Figure 6.4**

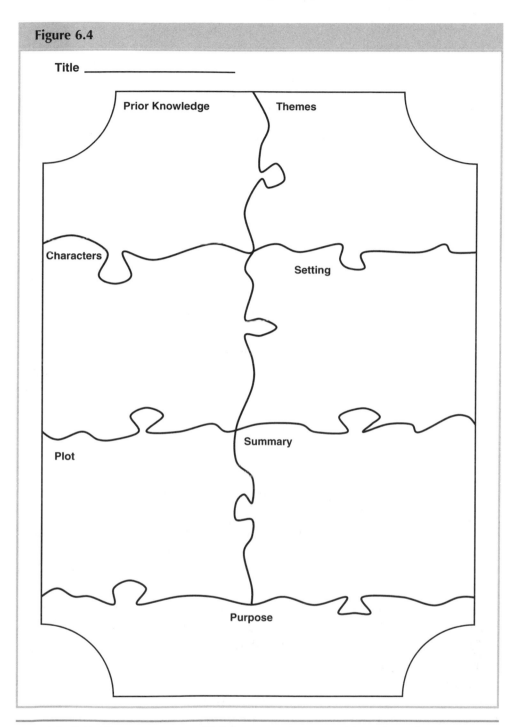

Title _____

Prior Knowledge

Themes

Characters

Setting

Plot

Summary

Purpose

strongly that two of the characters, Yingtao and Matthew, are building a friendship.

They share these ideas to support their thinking:

---

"When Matthew sees the fish in his friend's bathtub, he laughed at Yingtao, but it wasn't a mean laugh. Friends can laugh at one another and not get mad."

"Both boys didn't use the same words when talking about the bathroom. When Matthew asked to use the bathroom and not the toilet, Yingtao thought he would like to take a bath. Matthew thought this was so funny."

"Matthew was poor and didn't like to talk about being poor, but Yingtao made him feel better because Chinese people don't mind talking about being poor or rich."

---

These thoughts are not spontaneously shared by Richard's students. He first must use some prompts from Cooper and Kiger (2006). What message does this story teach about life? What evidence supports your thinking about the big idea?

As students synthesize ideas and information from texts, they consistently rely on other learned cognitive strategies. They activate their prior knowledge, make connections to their personal experiences, ask questions to clarify their thinking, evaluate their understanding of themes, refer to their mental images, and share their reflective thoughts in a safe, supportive environment.

---

In 2001, one of Benjamin Bloom's former students, Lorin Anderson, along with a group of cognitive psychologists, revised his work. Bloom created the Taxonomy of Educational Objectives for categorizing the level of abstraction of questions that commonly occur in educational settings. Bloom originally named the categories with nouns: knowledge, comprehension, application, analysis, synthesis, and evaluation. In order to reflect thinking as an active process, Anderson and his group renamed each level with a verb (Tankersley, 2005). Within this revision came the change of "synthesis" to "create" and upgrading this to the sixth level. Realizing that synthesizing text involves linking new information with prior knowledge or with multiple texts to develop a new idea, establishing a new way of thinking, or creating a new product of some type, Anderson's renaming is logical. Consequently, in order to be proficient thinkers, readers must be able to synthesize their thinking and make predictions based on prior knowledge.

Now that Jenn's students have a tangible example of synthesizing, she is ready to dive into the most critical phase of instruction, modeling. See Table 6.2.

*(Text Continues on Page 121)*

**Table 6.2**

| NCTE Standards: |
| --- |
| **1.** Students read a wide range of print and nonprint texts to build an understanding of texts, of themselves, and of the cultures of the United States and the world; to acquire new information; to respond to the needs and demands of society and the workplace; and for personal fulfillment. Among these texts are fiction and nonfiction, classic and contemporary works. |
| **3.** Students apply a wide range of strategies to comprehend, interpret, evaluate, and appreciate texts. They draw on their prior experience, their interactions with other readers and writers, their knowledge of word meaning and of other texts, their word identification strategies, and their understanding of textual features (e.g., sound-letter correspondence, sentence structure, context, graphics). |

| **Picture Book:** *Wilma Unlimited* by Kathleen Krull | | |
| --- | --- | --- |
| **Before** High ↕ Low | **Teacher** Read title and give a brief summary about the story. *Today I am going to read you a story entitled Wilma Unlimited. I am going to model good synthesizing skills that will help me to understand the story better. I want you to pay close attention to how I am thinking about what I am reading.* *When I select books to read I often read the back of the book where there is usually a summary of the plot so that I get a feeling for what the book will be about and also to see if it is about something that interests me.* *This book is a true story about a woman named Wilma Rudolph. Wilma was a very famous track and field runner who had a disease called polio. I run track and field in high school so I am immediately interested* | Activates prior knowledge, thinks about the shape activity and begins to create an idea. **Student** |

*(Continued)*

**Table 6.2** (Continued)

|  | | |
| --- | --- | --- |
| | *in reading this book, and also have prior knowledge to connect with.* | |
| | *Before I begin reading I am going to jot down my opinions and prior knowledge. As I mentioned earlier, synthesis includes combining two parts to understand the story better. These two parts are prior knowledge and story text. Opinion: Before Reading* (show on overhead): See Figures 6.5 and 6.6. *I know that Wilma Rudolph ran track and field. I also know that Wilma Rudolph had a disease called polio. I have definitely heard of this disease before and I believe that it is a disease contracted from an infection. I remember having to get shots to prevent polio when I was small. Although I don't know many particular facts about polio, I know that it is a serious disease that can cause paralysis of arms and legs, to the point that they can no longer function. Since I used to run track and field I know how tough the sport can be on the body. Therefore, I am doubtful that Wilma will be able to run well with her disease, and if she does run at all she will need to overcome huge obstacles and be very strong.* | |

| During High ↕ Low | **Teacher**<br>Begin reading text aloud.<br><br>*Now that I have written down my prior knowledge based upon my opinions, experiences, and knowledge I am ready to start reading. As I read I will be keeping track of what I am learning. Remember the second piece of synthesis requires us to build on our prior knowledge with information we learn through the text. I will keep track of the new information I learn in the second column of the overhead entitled "New Ideas: During Reading."*<br><br>*I have all pages that I reference on the overhead marked with Post-it notes. As I come to a marked page I will mention my thinking, otherwise I will read through the story at this time. I have only included marked pages below, along with my script.*<br><br>Page 1: *Wow, it surprises me that Wilma was born prematurely and it is important that everyone thought she would not make it to her first birthday and did. I am going to take note of this.*<br><br>Page 3: *I think it is important that Wilma contracted polio when she was just five years old. It makes me sad that back then there was no cure for polio. I am going to write this down as well. It must have been very hard for Wilma to face that this disease was incurable and also that everyone believed she would never walk again.*<br><br>Page 4: *Wow, Wilma had twenty-one brothers and sisters. She had a huge family. I wonder* | Activates prior knowledge and continues to gather information to create an evolving synthesis.<br><br><br><br><br><br><br><br><br><br><br><br><br><br><br><br><br><br><br><br><br><br><br><br><br><br><br><br><br><br><br><br><br><br><br><br><br><br><br><br><br><br><br><br><br><br><br><br><br><br><br><br><br><br><br><br><br><br><br><br><br>**Student** |

*(Continued)*

**Table 6.2** (Continued)

|  | | |
|---|---|---|
|  | *how this impacted her. I am going to take note of this, it is so amazing. It is also nice that her mother was willing to take her to a special hospital twice a week; Wilma's parents were really supportive.*<br><br>**Page 5:** *It must have been so hard for Wilma to see her brothers and sisters leave for school each morning, especially since she couldn't go with them. Wilma really hated being different. I think this is a turning point for Wilma. I am going to write this down so that I remember it later.*<br><br>**Page 12:** *I am so surprised that Wilma made it to the Olympics. There are so many good runners at the Olympics. Therefore her chances of winning a medal must have been small. I also can't imagine running on a sprained ankle. Wilma had so many obstacles to overcome.*<br><br>**Page 14:** *It must have been so motivating for her to hear so many people cheering her name. Wilma was really supported in her race.*<br><br>**Page 16:** *Wilma learned the power of concentration when she was fighting her disease. I remember when she was in the church she had to really concentrate so that she wouldn't fall down. This concentration that she learned helped her win the race for her team. Now that I have read this story it is my job to synthesize the two columns. One column is my prior knowledge and the other column is the new ideas I learned while* | |

reading. Remember synthesis includes combining my prior knowledge and newly learning information to come up with new ideas, thoughts, or opinions.

Show the students the synthesis statement that illustrates your synthesis of prior knowledge and newly acquired information. This statement will be on the overhead as well.

*To me this story illustrates that all people can overcome obstacles and be successful. Wilma was faced with many obstacles such as contracting an incurable disease and facing the doubts and disbelief of almost everyone she knew. However, Wilma had the support of her family and learned to believe in herself which in turn helped her to be successful. Through her struggles to overcome these odds she learned many important life lessons such as the importance of dedication, and concentration. Today she serves as a model of a true hero who inspires people to believe that they can succeed despite all odds against them.*

*This illustrates my new ideas after reading the story* Wilma Unlimited. *Before reading the story I was doubtful Wilma would be able to run with polio; however, I learned through reading that she was able to because she believed in herself, was supported by her family and friends, and learned the significance of concentration and determination.*

*(Continued)*

**Table 6.2** (Continued)

| | | |
|---|---|---|
| **After** | High ↕ Low | *Let's review our first activity.*<br><br>Allow each group to show and explain their creation from the anticipatory set. Post each of these creations on the chalkboard so that the students can visually see the multitude of ideas.<br><br>*Now I want to show you my creation. I made a house out of the shapes.*<br><br>*As you can see we have many different designs and pictures. This is a great example of synthesis. Give each group the same information (same number and type of pieces).*<br><br>*Each group also had different people with different prior knowledge and ideas* (different colored pieces). *The different colors and members in each group represent the differences in prior knowledge and experiences which we activate when we read a text. However, the same shape of piece represents that the text is the same for each person. We compiled our prior knowledge and text into a synthesis statement or in this case a picture that represented the combination of these two elements. As you can see from the board, we have seven different synthesis statements, which is okay. We all think differently, have different prior experiences, and can interpret the text differently.*<br><br>*As we review my final synthesis of Wilma Rudolph, did my opinion change?*<br><br>Wait for student responses.<br><br>*How?*<br><br>Allow students to respond.<br><br>*Yes, if we clearly state our opinion/thoughts before we read a piece of text or multiple texts, we are able to see the evolution of our synthesis.* | Actively shares synthesis of the shape packets.<br><br><br><br><br><br><br><br><br><br><br><br><br><br><br><br><br><br><br><br><br><br><br><br><br><br><br><br><br><br><br><br><br><br><br><br><br><br><br><br><br><br><br>**Student** |

**Figure 6.5**

## Comprehension Strategy: Synthesizing

| Opinion: Before Reading | New Ideas: During Reading |
|---|---|
| 1. Wilma Rudolph was a very famous track and field runner.<br><br>2. Wilma contracted polio in her leg when she was very young.<br><br>3. Polio is a disease contracted through an infection that can permanently lead to paralysis of arms and/or legs.<br><br>4. Since I ran track and field when I was in high school, I understand that the sport is very physically demanding and requires extensive conditioning and strength.<br><br>5. Wilma Rudolph must have overcome tremendous obstacles to regain strength in her leg and be able to run competitively. | 1. Wilma was born prematurely and was not expected to survive to her 1st birthday.<br><br>2. Wilma contracted polio when she was five years old and there was no cure for the disease at this time.<br><br>3. Almost everyone who knew Wilma believed that she would never walk again.<br><br>4. Wilma had very supportive parents, and many brothers and sisters who encouraged her.<br><br>5. Wilma hated being different from her friends and set her mind to fighting her disease.<br><br>6. In the Olympics, her chances of winning the gold medal were small; she even twisted her ankle when she first arrived at the Olympics.<br><br>7. Wilma was supported at the Olympics by spectators and fans.<br><br>8. Wilma learned important life lessons through her struggle to overcome polio, such as the power of concentration that in turn led her to win the race. |

**My Synthesis:** The story of Wilma Rudolph illustrates that all people can overcome the obstacles put in front of them and be successful. Wilma was faced with many obstacles such as contracting an incurable disease and facing the doubts and disbelief of almost everyone she knew. However, Wilma had the support of her family and learned to believe in herself, which in turn helped her to be successful. Through her struggles to overcome these odds she learned many important life lessons such as the importance of dedication and concentration. Today she serves as a model of a true hero who inspires people to believe that they can succeed despite all odds against them.

As Jenn reflects on her lesson she feels that her modeling demonstrated a good example of how to read text and make notes while reading. She shares her reflection:

---

I feel that I planned the lesson so that it connected the anticipatory set with the modeling and closure. I was also happy when I met with my cooperating teacher and she told me that the unit the class had just started reading was a unit on people who dare to be different. This lesson fit perfectly into her unit! Indeed, when I introduced Wilma Rudolph, the students shouted and cheered that they had heard of her, which was great because they then had prior knowledge and were able to focus more on my modeling. The students really enjoyed the anticipatory set of the lesson, because it gave them the opportunity to be cooperative and creative. They were so excited when they got to share their pictures; their creativity and uniqueness were exactly what I had hoped would happen with the anticipatory set.

I was hoping that I would be able to get some sort of body language signaling that the students made the connection between the synthesizing strategy and the anticipatory set. I did not feel completely confident that they made the connection; however, I really tried to reiterate that each synthesis statement can be different. I am hoping that the students made the connections that I wanted them to; however, I think I should have planned an activity for closure that would have given me some sort of confidence and tangible evidence that the connections were made. I feel that repetition is really important in the elementary grades because the students are learning new strategies that they have never used before and will later be required to apply them in many different subjects.

---

**Table 6.3**

---

NCTE Standards:

**1.** Students read a wide range of print and nonprint texts to build an understanding of texts, of themselves, and of the cultures of the United States and the world; to acquire new information; to respond to the needs and demands of society and the workplace; and for personal fulfillment. Among these texts are fiction and nonfiction, classic and contemporary works.

**3.** Students apply a wide range of strategies to comprehend, interpret, evaluate, and appreciate texts. They draw on their prior experience, their interactions with other readers and writers, their knowledge of word meaning and of other texts, their word identification strategies, and their understanding of textual features (e.g., sound-letter correspondence, sentence structure, context, graphics).

**Picture Book:** *Life in the Ghetto* by Anika Thomas

| Before High ↕ Low | **Teacher** *Today we are going to read* Life in the Ghetto *to continue learning about visualizing.* *Yesterday, I modeled for you. Today is a We Do day! I am going to give each of you a clipboard and an organizer to record your opinions and any new ideas. When I am reading today, I will stop along the way and give you a chance to record your notes.* *At the end of today's read aloud, I will ask each of you to review your notes and share your synthesis with your neighbors.* *Today's book,* Life in the Ghetto, *was written by a 13-year-old girl. Anika shares the life she lives in a tough, inner-city neighborhood in Pittsburgh, PA.* *Before I read, I want you to form an idea about* Life in the Ghetto. *Use your organizer to record your opinions in the left column.* See Figure 6.6. *Record as many ideas that you have.* Allow time for students to think and record. | Activates prior knowledge, thinks about the title and the book's summary to create an idea about *Life in the Ghetto.*

**Student** |

**Table 6.3** (Continued)

| | | |
|---|---|---|
| **During** High ↕ Low | Begin reading. Pause at the end of page 7. *Take some time to think about Anika's introduction. Raise your hand if you have a new idea forming in your mind. Great, write that new idea in the right hand column of your organizer.* Allow time for students to record their ideas. *The next section that I would like to read to you today has a subtitle, "My Mom Minds Her Own Business." Think about what this means to you. What do you know about minding your own business? Write your idea in the left column, under your first opinion.* Allow students time to record their idea. Read the next section, stopping after, "It is all I am used to, but I see it for what it is. I want out!" *Take some time to think about Anika's description. Raise your hand if you have a new idea forming in your mind. Great, write that new idea in the right hand column of your organizer.* Allow time for students to record their ideas. *The next section I want to share with you today has a subtitle, "Rats, Roaches, and Mice!" Think about what this means to you. What do you know about rats, roaches, and mice? Write your idea in the left column.* Allow students time to record their idea. Read the next section, stopping after, "If I do, I'll move my family out of here first thing!" | Student examples: *I think Anika's neighborhood is very different from my neighborhood.* *It would be very hard to have fun with your friends if you couldn't play outside without your parents.* *My cousin might die if she lived in Anika's apartment. She is allergic to roaches.* *I feel sorry for Anika. She has many mean kids in her school. I am glad I don't have so many mean kids.* |

| | | | |
|---|---|---|---|
| | | *Take some time to think about Anika's description of her apartment. Raise your hand if you have a new idea forming in your mind. Great, write that new idea in the right hand column of your organizer.* Allow time for students to record their ideas.<br><br>*The next section I want to share with you today has a subtitle, "Kids Can Be Really Mean!" Think about what this means to you. What do you know about how kids treat one another? Write your idea in the left column.*<br><br>Allow students time to record their idea.<br><br>Read the next section, stopping at the bottom of page 18.<br><br>*Take some time to think about Anika's experiences with other children. Raise your hand if you have a new idea forming in your mind. Great, write that new idea in the right hand column of your organizer.*<br><br>Allow time for students to record their ideas. | |
| **After** | High ↑ ↓ Low | Have students meet in small groups to share new ideas. Take notes on how their ideas changed or did not change as Anika's story progressed.<br><br>Finally, assess the students' learning by asking the following questions:<br><br>*How did your idea of life in the ghetto change?*<br><br>*Why is it important to stop and reflect on what we read?*<br><br>*What happens to our ideas as we gather more information from the story?*<br><br>**Teacher** | **Student**<br>Actively engages in the small group discussions to share the similarities and differences among new ideas of peers. Responds to the teacher's questions to demonstrate understanding of this cognitive strategy. |

**Figure 6.6**

| Opinion: Before Reading | New Ideas: During Reading |
|---|---|
|  |  |

Meanwhile, in Pam's fifth grade classroom, she learns that her students are ready to enter the We Do phase (supportive joint practice or scaffolding) of synthesizing instruction. She gathered evidence from her previous modeling lessons that her students now understand what it means to synthesize. Her students' comments include:

"When you synthesize, the author wrote so well that you learned something new which caused you to change your original thoughts," and

"I think it's easier to synthesize when you have some prior knowledge about a topic."

Since Pam teaches in a predominantly suburban to rural area, she wants to broaden her students' understanding of the lives of other kids in nearby communities. Many of her students have watched the news and heard about ghettos. She feels they had enough prior knowledge about a ghetto to synthesize Anika Thomas's book, *Life in the Ghetto* (see Table 6.3 on page 118).

After Pam's lesson, it is evident that Anika Thomas's first-hand experiences are so powerful that Pam's students changed their thinking and created powerful synthesis statements.

**Table 6.4**

| NCTE Standards: |
|---|

**1.** Students read a wide range of print and nonprint texts to build an understanding of texts, of themselves, and of the cultures of the United States and the world; to acquire new information; to respond to the needs and demands of society and the workplace; and for personal fulfillment. Among these texts are fiction and nonfiction, classic and contemporary works.

**3.** Students apply a wide range of strategies to comprehend, interpret, evaluate, and appreciate texts. They draw on their prior experience, their interactions with other readers and writers, their knowledge of word meaning and of other texts, their word identification strategies, and their understanding of textual features (e.g., sound-letter correspondence, sentence structure, context, graphics).

**Picture Book:** Students self-select their texts at the listening center. See Resources for suggested titles.

| | | |
|---|---|---|
| **Before** High ↕ Low | *Remember when we read together _____, _____, _____, and _____ and we shared our synthesis statements with one another. As you independently read _____, you may want to take notes on either of the organizers we have used in order to develop your synthesis statement. This way, I can see and read your creations.* | Self-selects a piece of literature to read.<br><br>**Student** |
| **During** High ↕ Low | In between small group instruction and/or during transition time, evaluate the students' use of prior knowledge and textual information to synthesize. Make sure prior knowledge is appropriate and the evidence is supportive, coaching the student during independent conferences. Also, monitor the changing of the synthesis as new information is learned. You may want to make anecdotal notes for when and for whom this process breaks down. You will use these notes to adjust small group instruction.<br>**Teacher** | Reads _____ and records a synthesis statement.<br><br><br>**Student** |

*(Continued)*

**Table 6.4** (Continued)

| | | | **Student** |
|---|---|---|---|
| **After** | High ↕ Low | During transition time, ask for volunteers to share their thinking and synthesis statements. | Orally shares thinking and synthesis statement. (Statements can be shared on an enlarged puzzle organizer to reinforce the various statements that can be synthesized from one piece of text.) |
| | | **Teacher** | |

Realizing many of her students need to spend more time in the We Do phase, Pam continues to use Thomas's book and provide guided practice instruction where needed. As her fifth graders show more evidence of clearly synthesizing the author's information, Pam gradually moves them into the independent application. Pam knows when she moves students too quickly, they are unable to sustain this higher level of thinking and don't create new ways of thinking. She pulls these students back into her guided practice group until she finds stronger evidence.

⎯⎯⎯⎯ ⚬ ⎯⎯⎯⎯

After many lessons of modeling, Mary Margaret decides her sixth graders are ready to accept more responsibility for their learning. As she moves into the independent application phase of instruction, she asks her students to synthesize the text in order to determine the underlying theme. In order to maintain a bit of control during the You Do phase, Mary Margaret supplies students with the texts, Jane Yolen and Barbara Cooney's *Letting Swift River Go* and Anna Quindlen's *Homeless*.

As her students become engaged in these texts, she provides some thinking questions to guide their synthesizing:

- How do the authors' feelings change?
- What is each author's message?

- What messages do these texts teach you?
- What do you know about homelessness after reading these texts?

Mary Margaret finds that her students are able to discuss their responses in small groups quite well. However, she soon realizes that they need more guided practice as they synthesize these thoughts and put them into personal written responses. Accordingly, Mary Margaret next has her students meet with her in small groups to share strategies on how to gather appropriate information from the text as they read. She notes that her students are not being as active during reading as they need to be. Mary Margaret revisits her questions with her students:

- How do the authors' feelings change?
- What is each author's message?
- What messages do these texts teach you?
- What do you know about homelessness after reading these texts?

Mary Margaret recognizes the need to revisit the sustaining strategy of gathering information in order to become more active synthesizers. She separates her students into small groups to provide more guided practice. This revisit to guided practice did not last as long as her first phase of guided practice instruction; her students are able to move back into the independent application phase with much more ease, since she has spent the time to reteach them how to gather information to support their syntheses. Consequently, her students are able to accurately summarize the text with their prior knowledge, by including ideas and themes relevant to the text, along with other readers' ideas and syntheses.

Synthesis is about organizing the different pieces to create a mosaic, or a meaning and a beauty, greater than the sum of each shiny piece (Keene & Zimmerman, 1997). See Table 6.4 on page 123.

---

## SUMMARY

- Synthesizing integrates new knowledge with prior knowledge.
- Proficient readers keenly revise their synthesis as they read.
- Proficient readers synthesize to better understand what they have read.
- Synthesis statements prepare students for engaging in oral discussions.

As you conclude your thinking adventure, stop and reflect . . .

**Table 6.5**

| Make your thinking visible . . . | | |
|---|---|---|
| **Reflection Questions:** | *How will you challenge yourself to develop a new idea? How effectively do my students integrate new knowledge with prior knowledge to deepen their understanding?* | |
| **Modeling Through Think Aloud** — High ↕ Low | **Teacher** | **Student** |
| **Guided Practice** — High ↕ Low | **Teacher** | **Student** |
| **Independent Application** — High ↕ Low | **Teacher** | **Student** |

# 7 Conclusion

## *The You-Do Phase of Making the Invisible Visible*

*Independence in reading is the ultimate goal of reading instruction.*

—Peter Afflerbach

As you begin to bring life to your thinking, you will make these invisible strategies visible for your readers. In the beginning, your readers need to see and hear all of your thoughts. As you move them through the gradual release model, their thinking will come to life and they will need less support but more observation from you. The BDA framework will guide your planning to ensure that you meet their needs through the entire lesson. Consequently, you reflect, asking, "What can my students do today that I can build upon tomorrow?" Here are five simple steps that will guide your independent application for planning and instruction.

Step 1: Assess student strengths and needs by knowing and understanding your state's standards.

Step 2: Analyze student work samples, anecdotal notes, and student conversations.

Step 3: Match the student's understandings and misconceptions with your state's objectives.

Step 4: Determine what the child is able to do independently and what is interfering with the child's progress.

Step 5: Prioritize and select objectives which will move the child toward independence.

## SELECT APPROPRIATE RESOURCES

When considering text selection, recognize the readers' interests and background knowledge, think about the text's characteristics and content, and the available learning opportunities that will support the established learning goals.

- Plan your instruction on the BDA framework.
- Select which phase of instruction will support the child's learning.
- Practice your Think Aloud.
- Provide appropriate instruction.
- During the I Do phase, independently model the strategy expectations as students do not interfere with your Think Aloud.
- During the We Do phase, as the students demonstrate some competency, negotiate and match the reading material to the student needs as you scaffold the students' learning in the We Do phase. Students will begin to actively participate in the Think Aloud.
- During the You Do phase, allow the students to regulate their learning as they choose their material.

# Afterword

## A Framework for Literacy Instruction in Your K–6 Classroom

*Ellin Keene*

I have never been asked to write an "afterword" for a professional book, so I wondered, as I read the chapter on making the invisible visible, how I would approach the task—how could I possibly add anything of value to readers satiated with dozens of ideas and concepts they've just read? In this book, Divonna and Joy present a solid instructional model based on years of research and provide numerous teaching tactics to help teachers, particularly those new to the profession, imagine how comprehension strategy instruction might actually look and sound in the elementary classroom. How could I possibly add to that constellation of knowledge?

It wasn't until rereading Chapters 4 and 5 that I realized the most I could hope to add to a book as focused and practical as this one is to help readers look beyond it. I could propose a set of ideas about what might come next in the readers' quests to fully understand reading comprehension instruction. It was Divonna and Joy themselves who made this clear to me. They begin this book by recalling a personal fifth grade learning experience—in this case, a math teacher—and go on to articulate their extraordinary learning alongside the teachers and children with whom they currently work. Without saying so, they make a strong statement about their own vibrant, ongoing learning. These authors know that when you finish a book like this one, it makes you thirsty for more—you want to probe the ideas more deeply, consider other perspectives, discuss the ideas with colleagues, refine and revise the concepts in your own classroom. In short, a book like this makes you want to learn more.

So, in the spirit of ongoing learning, of constantly revising and refining ideas and in the spirit of experimenting, fooling around with and reshaping what we think we know, I propose that you, the reader, consider the following tasks.

Capitalize on the concrete lessons presented here by creating your own, original Think Alouds for children.

Create original ways to make the strategies concrete and understandable to children. For example, instead of unpacking a suitcase, think about how you might demonstrate what schema or background knowledge is and how it works for children to understand better.

Continue to apply the strategies Divonna and Joy describe here to your own reading, as they do in the introduction, carefully considering how your own metacognitive mind makes meaning.

Explore the notion of scaffolding by imagining the kind of scaffolding that each of your own students might need in order to apply these strategies in progressively more difficult text.

Use the BDA framework to create your own units of study focusing on each of the comprehension strategies. Experiment with different lengths of study on each strategy—observe how much deeper your students' comprehension reaches.

Experiment with various genres for each strategy—think aloud about how readers use each strategy differently in the context of different genres. For example, how does a reader question differently in nonfiction than fiction or poetry?

Use the strategy organizers and instructional planning tools, such as column charts, presented in this book in other disciplines. How might you use a KWL chart in science or math? For example, talk with your colleagues to discover how they are adapting the ideas in this book and experiment with their revisions as well as those in this book. Explore the research Joy and Divonna cite to understand the concepts they discuss more deeply—they provide an invaluable set of references in this book and it would be a missed opportunity not to follow some of their references into better understanding the theories that underlie their ideas. It's solid as a rock and the finest teachers understand not just what to do in the classroom, but why they do it.

Avoid the rut—the comprehension strategies provide a common language with which children and adults can define and describe their thinking, but they should never become routine, basalized, or drudgery for children.

Help students understand why you're focusing on comprehension strategies. The strategies are tools because readers use them—nothing more. The goal is not to have students using the strategies but to have students use the strategies in order to comprehend more deeply. Talk to your students about what they understand using the strategies that they might not have understood by reading without conscious use of those strategies.

Blaze your own path. As Divonna and Joy will tell you, there is no one right way to teach comprehension strategies, and they say clearly in the introduction that they adapt their approaches based on the observed needs of their students.

Teachers have so much to keep in mind, so many tasks to juggle. Life for a teacher, particularly those new to the profession, can be overwhelming, to say the least. Teachers as skilled as Divonna, Joy, and the others with whom they've learned from in order to write this book know that we can take all the demands too seriously and become too easily overwhelmed with "should haves" and "could haves" and miss the joy in teaching and learning. Children are joyful and curious and they are intellectual sponges—the best teachers remember this in everything they do and stop themselves from becoming too intent on their own purposes and lessons that they forget to attend to children's needs and interests.

I've decided that I love the idea of an afterword! How lucky I've been to get to read this book in draft form and then think ahead on the reader's behalf—what might you pursue next to go from being a good teacher to a superb one; what might you want to consider in order to become even more confident and well-informed; how might you adapt the great ideas Divonna and Joy share to meet the specific needs of the children with whom you're lucky enough to work? It's a lot of fun to think into the future, to look at the horizon rather than the path immediately in front of you. You know, you really ought to try it sometime!

---

NOTE: Ellin Oliver Keene is the coauthor of *Mosaic of Thought: Teaching Comprehension in a Reader's Workshop* (1997) and the forthcoming *To Understand*.

# Resource A

*Framework Template*

**NCTE Standards:**

**1.** Students read a wide range of print and nonprint texts to build an understanding of texts, of themselves, and of the cultures of the United States and the world; to acquire new information; to respond to the needs and demands of society and the workplace; and for personal fulfillment. Among these texts are fiction and nonfiction, classic and contemporary works.

**3.** Students apply a wide range of strategies to comprehend, interpret, evaluate, and appreciate texts. They draw on their prior experience, their interactions with other readers and writers, their knowledge of word meaning and of other texts, their word identification strategies, and their understanding of textual features (e.g., sound-letter correspondence, sentence structure, context, graphics).

**Guiding Question:**

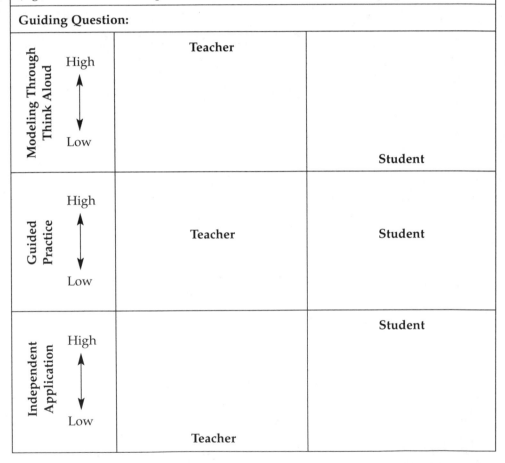

# Resource B

## *Thinking Organizers*

Name: _____

Visualizing

Changing Mental Images as We Read

We read: _____

| My image before reading . . . | and now . . . |
|---|---|
| and now . . . | and now . . . |

# Resource C

## Picture Book Reference Lists

| Determining Importance | |
|---|---|
| Author | Title |
| Bartoletti, Susan | *Growing Up in Coal Country* |
| Curlee, Lynn | *Rushmore* |
| Freedman, Russell | *Cowboys of the Wild West* |
| Freedman, Russell | *Lincoln: A Photobiography* |
| Freedman, Russell | *Indian Chiefs* |
| Freedman, Russell | *Immigrant Kids* |
| Fritz, Jean | *SHH! We're Writing the Constitution* |
| Fritz, Jean | *What's the Big Idea Ben Franklin* |
| James, Simon | *Dear Mr. Blueberry* |
| Keenan, Sheila | *Encyclopedia of Women in the United States* |
| Lundell, Margo (editor) | *Through My Eyes Ruby Bridges* |
| Martin, Jacqueline | *Snowflake Bentley* |
| Mochizuki, Ken | *Baseball Saved Us* |
| Pinkney, Andrea Davis | *Duke Ellington* |
| Simon, Seymour | *Whales* |
| Simon, Seymour | *Sharks* |
| Spedden, Daisy | *Polar, the Titanic Bear* |
| Williams, Sherley Anne | *Working Cotton* |
| Yolen, Jane | *Letting Swift River Go* |
|  | *iOpeners* |
|  | *Rosen Real Readers* |

| Inferring | |
|---|---|
| **Author** | **Title** |
| Anderson, William | *River Boy: The Story of Mark Twain* |
| Avi | *Poppy* |
| Barron, T. A. | *The Lost Years of Merlin* |
| Baylor, Byrd | *The Table Where Rich People Sit* |
| Bruchac, Joseph | *Four Ancestors: The Shinning Mountain* |
| Bunting, Eve | *Dandelion* |
| Bunting, Eve | *The Wall* |
| Bunting, Eve | *Jin Woo* |
| Bunting, Eve | *How Many Days to America* |
| Bunting, Eve | *Secret Place* |
| Bunting, Eve | *The Bones of Fred McFee* |
| Eaton, Deb | *The Fox and the Crow* |
| Fleischman, Paul | *Bull Run* |
| Fleischman, Paul | *Dateline: Troy* |
| Fleischman, Paul | *Weslandia* |
| Hazen, Barbara Shook | *Tight Times* |
| Heard, Georgia (compiled) | *This Place I Know* |
| Heard, Georgia (compiled) | *Stars* |
| Hesse, Karen | *Out of the Dust* |
| Innocenti, Roberto | *Rose Blanche* |
| Lewis, Kim | *Floss* |
| L'Engle, Madeleine | *A Wrinkle in Time* |
| Mitchell, Margaree King | *Granddaddy's Gift* |
| Parks, Frances & Ginger | *The Royal Bee* |
| Parry, Florence | *The Day of Ahmed's Secre* |
| Polacco, Patricia | *The Keeping Quilt* |
| Polacco, Patricia | *Babushka's Doll* |
| Rylant, Cynthia | *An Angel for Solomon Singer* |
| Sachar, Louis | *Holes* |
| Sakai, Kimiko | *Sachiko Means Happiness* |

| Inferring | |
|---|---|
| **Author** | **Title** |
| Scieszka, Jon | *The Frog Prince...Continued* |
| Soto, Gary | *Too Many Tamales* |
| Teague, Mark | *Dear Mr. Larue: Letters From Obedience School* |
| Teague, Mark | *Detective Larue: Letters From Investigation* |
| Thermes, Jennifer | *When I Was Built* |
| Woodson, Jacqueline | *The Other Side* |
| Zolotow, Charlotte | *If You Listen* |

| Schemata | |
|---|---|
| **Author** | **Title** |
| Adler, David | *Lou Gehrig: The Luckiest Man* |
| Ballard, Robert | *Exploring the Titanic* |
| Creech, Sharon | *Walk Two Moons* |
| Fleischman, Paul | *Bull Run* |
| Fox, Mem | *Wilfrid Gordon McDonald Partridge* |
| Fox, Paula | *The Slave Dancer* |
| Garland, Sherry | *The Lotus Seed* |
| Hewett, Jean | *Rosalie* |
| Hoffman, Mary | *Amazing Grace* |
| Polacco, Patricia | *Chicken Sunday* |
| Polacco, Patricia | *Mrs. Katz and Tush* |
| Polacco, Patricia | *Thank You, Mr. Falker* |
| Rylant, Cynthia | *The Relatives Came* |
| Rylant, Cynthia | *When I Was Young in the Mountains* |
| Soto, Gary | *Neighborhood Odes* |
| Waber, Bernard | *Ira Sleeps Over* |
| Wild, Margaret | *Let the Celebrations Begin!* |

| Questioning | |
|---|---|
| **Author** | **Title** |
| Abercrombie, Barbara | *Charlie Anderson* |
| Adler, David A. | *Young Cam Jansen and the Double Beach Mystery* |
| Allsburg, Chris Van | *Just a Dream* |
| Allsburg, Chris Van | *The Wreck of the Zephyr* |
| Barbalet, Margaret | *The Wolf* |
| Berger, Melvin & Gilda | *Why Do Volcanoes Blow Their Tops?* |
| Bunting, Eve | *A Day's Work* |
| Bunting, Eve | *Fly Away Home* |
| Bunting, Eve | *How Many Days to America?* |
| Bunting, Eve | *The Wednesday Surprise* |
| Foreman, Michael | *War Boys* |
| George, Lindsay Barrett | *In the Snow: Who's Been Here* |
| Gerstein, Mordical | *The Man Who Walked Between the Towers* |
| Hoffman, Mary, & Binch, Caroline | *Amazing Grace* |
| Janeczko, Paul | *The Place My Words Are Looking For* |
| Kramer, Stephen | *Avalanche* |
| MacLachlan, Patricia | *The Sick Day* |
| McDonald, Megan | *The Potato Man* |
| McKee, David | *Elmer* |
| Mitchell, Margaree King | *Uncle Jed's Barbershop* |
| Olson, Steven P. | *The Trial of John T. Scopes* |
| Pearson, Tracey Campbell | *Where Does Joe Go?* |
| Polacco, Patricia | *Christmas Tapestry* |
| Polacco, Patricia | *I Can Hear the Sun* |
| Polacco, Patricia | *My Rotten Redheaded Older Brother* |
| Polacco, Patricia | *Pink and Say* |
| Polacco, Patricia | *The Bee Tree* |
| Reiss, Johanna | *The Upstairs Room* |

## Questioning

| Author | Title |
|---|---|
| Rylant, Cynthia | *Something Permanent* |
| Spinelli, Eileen | *Something to Tell the Grandcows* |
| Uchida, Yoshiko | *The Bracelet* |
| Welch, Catherine | *Children of the Civil Rights Era* |
| Wiles, Deborah | *Freedom Summer* |
| Yolen, Jane | *How Do Dinosaurs Say Good Night?* |
| Yolen, Jane | *Owl Moon* |
| Yolen, Jane | *Where Have the Unicorns Gone?* |

## Visualizing

| Author | Title |
|---|---|
| Allsburg, Chris Van | *The Wreck of the Zephyr* |
| Anderson, M. T. | *Me, All Alone, at the End of the World* |
| Begay, Shonto | *Ma'ii and Cousin Horned Toad: A Traditional Navajo Story* |
| Brandenberg, Aliki | *Painted Words/Spoken Memories: Marianthe's Story* |
| Brinkloe, Julie | *Fireflies* |
| Bunting, Eve | *Red Fox Running* |
| Bunting, Eve | *Butterfly House* |
| Coville, Bruce | *Half Human, "Water's Edge"* |
| Dalton, Annie | *The Starlight Princess and Other Princess Stories: The Frog Princess* |
| Dumont, Jean-Francois | *A Blue So Blue* |
| Fletcher, Ralph | *Twilight Comes Twice* |
| Hodges, Margaret | *Saint George and the Dragon* |
| Leewen, Jean | *Going West* |
| London, Jonathan | *Dream Weaver* |

*(Continued)*

(Continued)

| Visualizing | |
|---|---|
| **Author** | **Title** |
| London, Jonathan | *Puddles* |
| Mayer, Mercer | *Shibumi and the Kitemaker* |
| Mosel, Arlene | *Tikki Tikki Tembo* |
| Reiss, Mike | *Late for School* |
| Rossetti, Christina | *Fly Away, Fly Away Over the Sea and Other Poems for Children* |
| San Souci, Robert | *The Snow Wife* |
| San Souci, Robert | *Sukey and the Mermaid* |
| Sherman, Josepha | *Magic Hoof-beats: Horse Tales From Many Lands: Horses of Steppes* |
| Springer, Nancy | *Half Human, "Becoming"* |
| Ward, Helen, & Andrew, Ian | *The Boat* |
| Yolen, Jane | *Raising Yoder's Barn* |
| Zolotow, Charlotte | *The Seashore Book* |

| Synthesizing | |
|---|---|
| **Author** | **Title** |
| Aardema, Verna | *Why Mosquitoes Buzz in People's Ears* |
| Abells, Charra Byers | *The Children We Remember* |
| Alexander, Lloyd | *The Four Donkeys* |
| Babbit, Natalie | *Tuck Everlasting* |
| Bang, Molly | *The Grey Lady and the Strawberry Snatcher* |
| Banks, Kate | *And If the Moon Could Talk* |
| Brandenberg, Aliki | *Marianthe's story one & two—Spoken Memories/Painted Words* |
| Brown, Marcia | *Shadow* |
| Bunting, Eve | *Fly Away Home* |
| Bunting, Eve | *A Day's Work* |

| Synthesizing | |
|---|---|
| **Author** | **Title** |
| Cleary, Beverly | *Dear Mr. Henshaw* |
| Coerr, Eleanor | *Sadako and the Thousand Paper Cranes* |
| Cole, Joanna | *On the Ocean Floor* |
| Cole, Joanna | *In the Time of Dinosaurs* |
| Connell, Kate | *Colonial Life* |
| Connell, Kate | *Our New Life in America* |
| Connell, Kate | *The Spirit of a New Nation* |
| Crisp, Peter | *The Romans* |
| Crisp, Peter | *The Vikings* |
| Crisp, Peter | *Ancient Egypt* |
| Dahl, Roald | *Matilda* |
| Ehlert, Lois | *Red Leaf, Yellow Leaf* |
| Fox, Mem | *Koala Lou* |
| Fritz, Jean | *And Then What Happened, Paul Revere?* |
| Fritz, Jean | *Who's That Stepping on Plymouth Rock?* |
| Gibbons, Gail | *Monarch Butterfly* |
| Graham, Ian | *The Moon* |
| Graham, Ian | *Dinosaurs* |
| Graham, Ian | *Ponies* |
| Graham, Ian | *Bugs* |
| Halpren, Jerald | *A Look at Spiders* |
| Holt, Kimberly Willis | *My Louisiana Sky* |
| Honda, Tetsuya | *Wild Horse Winter* |
| Hooper, Roseanne | *Life on the Islands* |
| Hooper, Roseanne | *Life in the Woodlands* |
| Jenkins, Steve, & Page, Robin | *What Do You Do With a Tail Like This?* |
| Kellogg, Stephen | *Tall Tale Retelling Series: Johnny Appleseed* |
| Kitchen, Bert | *And So They Build* |

*(Continued)*

(Continued)

| Synthesizing | |
|---|---|
| **Author** | **Title** |
| Kroll, Steven | *Lewis and Clark: Explorers of the American West* |
| Krull, Kathleen | *Wilma Unlimited: How Wilma Rudolph Became the World's Fastest Woman* |
| Lawson, Barbara Spilman | *Newbridge Discovery Links Series: Exploring Caves* |
| Leaf, Minro | *I Hate You* |
| Littleda, Freva | *The Magic Plum Tree* |
| Llewellyn, Claire | *Paper* |
| Llewellyn, Claire | *Rubber* |
| Llewellyn, Claire | *Silk* |
| Llewellyn, Claire | *Plastic* |
| Macaulay, David | *Why the Chicken Crossed the Road* |
| MacLachlan, Patricia | *Sarah, Plain and Tall* |
| MacLeod, Elizabeth | *Lucy Maud Montgomery* |
| MacLeod, Elizabeth | *Alexander Graham Bell* |
| MacLeod, Elizabeth | *Helen Keller* |
| Martin, Alice | *The Glorious Flight* |
| Martin, C. L. G. | *Three Brave Women* |
| Mazer, Harry | *A Boy at War: A Novel of Pearl Harbor* |
| McDermott, Gerald | *Arrow to the Sun* |
| Michelson, Richard | *Did You Say Ghosts?* |
| Mochizuki, Ken | *Passage to Freedom* |
| Moehizuki, Ken | *Baseball Saved Us* |
| Moore, Kay | *If You Lived at the Time of the American Revolution* |
| Morgan, Sally | *Life in the Cities* |
| Moss, Marissa | *Rachel's Journal* |
| Newman, Leslea | *Belinda's Bouquet* |
| Ortiz, Annie, & Ferrell, Denise | *Jane Goodall: Living With Chimpanzees* |

| Synthesizing | |
|---|---|
| **Author** | **Title** |
| Otfinoski, Steven | *Who Needs Weeds* |
| Paulsen, Gary | *Hatchet* |
| Polacco, Patricia | *Pink and Say* |
| Rosen, Sydney | *Can You Hitch a Ride on a Comet?* |
| Rosen, Sydney | *Where Does the Moon Go?* |
| Rylant, Cynthia | *Missing May* |
| Say, Allen | *El Chino* |
| Scieszka, Jon | *Squids Will Be Squids* |
| Selsam, Millicent | *Questions and Answers About Horses* |
| Siberell, Anne | *Bravo! Brava! A Night at the Opera: Behind the Scenes, With Composers, Cast, and Crew* |
| Spinelli, Jerry | *My Daddy and Me* |
| Steptoe, John | *Daddy Is a Monster . . . Sometimes* |
| Woodruff, Elvira | *The Memory Coat* |
| Yolen, Jane | *Encounter* |

# References

Anderson R. C., & Pearson, P. D. (1984). A schema-theoretic view of basic processes in reading comprehension. In P. D. Pearson (Ed.), *Handbook of reading research* (pp. 255–291). New York: Longman.

Armbruster, B., & Anderson, T. H. (1984). Studying. In P. D. Pearson, R. Barr, L. Kamil, & P. B. Mosenthal (Eds.), *Handbook of reading research* (Vol. 3, pp. 657–679). New York: Longman.

Barclay, K. D. (1990). Constructing meaning: An integrated approach to teaching reading. *Intervention in School and Clinic, 26(2),* 84–91.

Block, C., Gambrell, L., & Pressley, M. (2002). *Improving comprehension instruction: Advances in research, theory, and classroom practice.* San Francisco, CA: Jossey-Bass.

Block, C. C., & Pressley, M. (2002). *Comprehension instruction research-based practices.* New York: Guilford.

Brinkloe, J. (1986). *Fireflies.* New York: Aladdin.

Brisson, P. (1998). *The summer my father was ten.* Honesdale, PA: Boyds Mill Press.

Brown, A. L., Armbruster, B., & Baker, L. (1986). The role of metacognition in reading and studying. In J. Orasanu (Ed.), *Reading comprehension: From research to practice* (pp. 49–75). Hillsdale, NJ: Erlbaum.

Bunting, E. (1995). *Dandelions.* New York: Harcourt.

Carpenter, S. (1998). *The three billy goats gruff.* New York: Scholastic.

Cooney, B. (1982). *Miss Rumphius.* New York: Penguin Putnam.

Cooper, J. D. and Kiger, N. (2006). *Literacy: Helping children construct meaning.* New York: Houghton Mifflin.

Dole, J. A., Duffy, G. G., Roehler, L. R., & Pearson, P. D. (1991). Moving from the old to the research on reading comprehension instruction. *Review of Educational Research, 61,* 239–264.

Duncan, L. (2000). *I walk at night.* New York: Viking.

Earle, S. A. (1999). *Dive! My adventures in the deep frontier.* New York: Scholastic.

Farr, R. (2002). Presentation: SOMIRAC.

Flavell, J. (1979). Metacognition and cognitive monitoring: A new area of cognitive-developmental inquiry. *American Psychologist, 34,* 906–911.

Fountas, I. C. & Pinnell, G. S. (2001). *Guiding readers and writers grades 3–6: Teaching comprehension, genre, and content literacy.* Portsmouth, NH: Heinemann.

Fredericks, A. D. (1986). Mental imagery activities to improve comprehension. *The Reading Teacher, 40,* 78–81.

Garner, R. (1988). *Metacognition and reading comprehension.* Norwood, NJ: Ablex.

Harvey, S., & Goudvis, A. (2000). *Strategies that work: Teaching comprehension to enhance understanding.* Portland, ME: Stenhouse.

Hoose, P. & H. (1998). *Hey little ant.* New York: Tricycle Press.

Hoyt, L. (2000). *Snapshots: Literacy lessons up close.* Portsmouth, NH: Heinemann.

Hoyt, L. (2005). *Spotlight on comprehension.* Portsmouth, NH: Heinemann.

Keene, E., & Zimmerman, S. (1997). *Mosaic of thought.* Portland, NH: Heinemann.

Knuth, R. A., & Jones, B. F. (1991). *What research says about reading.* Retrieved 12/20, 2004 from http://www.ncrel.org/sdrs/areas/stw esys/str read.htm

Krull, K. (2000). *Wilma unlimited: How Wilma Rudolph became the fastest woman.* Orlando, FL: Voyager Books.

Kucan, L., & Beck, I. L. (1997). Thinking aloud and reading comprehension research: Inquiry, instruction, and social interaction. *Review of Educational Research, 67(3),* 271–299.

Langer, J. A. (1995). *Envisioning literature, literary understanding and literature instruction.* New York: Teacher College Press.

Lipson, M., & Wixson, K. (2003). *Assessment & instruction of reading and writing difficult: An interactive approach.* New York: Longman.

Mazer, A. (1994). *The salamander room.* New York: Dragonfly.

Miller, D. (2002). *Reading with meaning.* Portland, ME: Stenhouse.

Namioka, L., & De Kiefte, K. (1992). *Yang the youngest and his terrible ear.* New York: Houghton Mifflin.

Nazario, S. (2006). *Enrique's journey: The story of a boy's dangerous odyssey to reunite with his mother.* New York: Random House.

Nolen, J. (1998). *Harvey potter's balloon farm.* New York: HarperTrophy.

Polacco, P. (1998). *Thank you, Mr. Falker.* New York: Philomel Books.

Pressley, M., Borkowski, J. G., & Schneider, W. (1987). Good strategy users coordinate metacognition, strategy use and knowledge. In R. Basta & G. Whitehurst (Eds.), *Annals of Child Development, 4,* 89–129.

Quindlen, A. (2002). *Blessings.* New York: Random House.

Reutzel, R., Camperell, K., & Smith, J. (2002). Helping struggling readers make sense of reading. In C. Collins-Block, L. B. Gambrell, & M. Pressley (Eds.), *Improving comprehension instruction: Advances in research, theory, and classroom practice.* San Francisco, CA: Jossey-Bass.

Routman, R. (2003). *Reading essentials: The specifics you need to teach reading well.* Portsmouth, NH: Heinemann.

Rylant, C. (1996). *An angel for Solomon Singer.* New York: Orchard Paperbacks.

Shannon, D. (1998). *A bad case of stripes.* New York, NY: Blue Sky Press.

Short, K. G., Harste, J., & Burke, C. (1996). *Creating classrooms for authors and inquirers* (2nd ed). Portsmouth, NH: Heinemann.

Stead, T. (2005). *Reality checks: Teaching reading comprehension with non-fiction K–5.* York, ME: Stenhouse.

Tankersley, K. (2005). *Literacy strategies for grades 4–12: Reinforcing the threads of reading.* Alexandria, VA: Association for Supervision and Curriculum Development.

Thomas, S. M. (1995). *Putting the world to sleep.* New York: Houghton Mifflin.

Vacca, R. T., & Vacca, J. L. (2002). *Content area reading: Literacy and learning across the curriculum.* Boston: Allyn & Bacon.

Van Allsburg, C. (1984). *The mysteries of Harris Burdick*. New York: Houghton Mifflin.

Van Allsburg, C. (1998). *Two bad ants*. New York, NY: Houghton Mifflin.

Vygotzky, L. S. (1978). *Mind in society: The development of higher psychological processes*. Cambridge, MA: Harvard University Press.

Wiggins, G. P., & McTighe, J. (2005). *Understanding by design*. Alexandria, VA: Association for Supervision and Curriculum Development.

Wilhelm, J. D. (2001a). *Improving comprehension with think-aloud strategies*. New York, NY: Scholastic.

Wilhelm, J. D. (2001b). *Strategic reading: Guiding students to lifelong literacy 6–12*. Portsmouth, NH: Heinemann.

Wood, A. (1984). *The napping house*. New York: Harcourt Brace.

Zemelman, S., Daniels, H., & Hyde, A. (2005). *Best practice: Today's standards for teaching and learning in America's schools*. Portsmouth, NH: Heinemann.

# Index

Note: References followed by *fig* indicate an illustrated figure; followed by *t* indicate a table.

**CORWIN PRESS**

The Corwin Press logo—a raven striding across an open book—represents the union of courage and learning. Corwin Press is committed to improving education for all learners by publishing books and other professional development resources for those serving the field of PreK–12 education. By providing practical, hands-on materials, Corwin Press continues to carry out the promise of its motto: **"Helping Educators Do Their Work Better."**